# THE NEW TESTAMENT

# THE NEW TESTAMENT

*History, Literature, Religion*

GERD THEISSEN

*Translated by*
JOHN BOWDEN

T & T CLARK
*A Continuum imprint*
LONDON • NEW YORK

T&T CLARK LTD

*A Continuum imprint*

The Tower Building          15 East 26th Street
11 York Road               New York 10010
London SE1 7NX, UK              USA

www.continuumbooks.com

Authorized English translation of Gerd Theissen,
*Das Neue Testament. Geschichte, Literatur, Religion*

Copyright © Verlag C. H. Beck oHG, Munich 2002


Translation copyright © John Bowden, 2003

First published 2003
Reprinted 2003


ISBN 0 567 08191 5 PB


British Library Cataloguing-in-Publication Data
A catalogue record for this book is available from the British Library

Typeset by Waverley Typesetters, Galashiels
Printed and bound in Great Britain by The Bath Press, Bath

# Contents

# Preface

The New Testament is a fundamental text of human history. With its help Christianity has shaped the behaviour and experiences of many men and women over 2,000 years. By reading it, from ancient times members of other religions have gained information about the foundations of Christianity. Only for about 300 years has it been subjected to scholarly investigation, often with sharp historical criticism that has confused the church and theology and has become a characteristic of modern culture.

Over this period many issues have been clarified. Today we know very much more about these twenty-seven short writings from a little religious sub-culture in the Roman empire than ever before. Nevertheless, they risk being forgotten – partly because the link with the Christian history which they have influenced has been broken, partly because many of our educated contemporaries come from other religious and cultural traditions, and partly because the results of historical-critical research are so complex that many people are deterred from trying to grasp them.

Consequently this short introduction to the New Testament sets out to sum up as briefly as possible, for anyone who is interested, the most important features of the New Testament. Information is given about each individual writing in the New Testament and at the same time an overall picture is given of the New Testament, its history, literature and religion.

This overall picture follows three ongoing lines. There is a literary line which looks at the two basic forms of the New Testament, letter and gospel, which came into being separately and were brought together for the first time in the Johannine writings. Then there is a historical line along which a renewal movement within Judaism gained its independence and became a separate religion, detached from its mother religion. Finally there is a theological line which traces the tension that came about as the result of the worship of an executed man as God in a religion which had emerged from Judaism. As a result the monotheism of Judaism was deeply transformed.

Of course other New Testament scholars will differ with the presentation of some of the aspects of my account. And as the description is so short, I can only give my reasons very briefly. But the picture presented here does claim to be free from extreme theses.

The English edition of this book is a thoroughly revised version of a short book *Das Neue Testament* which appeared in German in spring 2002. I am particularly grateful to John Bowden for his suggestion that this book should be published in English in its revised form and for translating it, and to T&T Clark for publishing it.

GERD THEISSEN
Heidelberg, June 2002

# Abbreviations

| | |
|---|---|
| Acts | Acts of the Apostles |
| *Ant.* | Josephus, *Jewish Antiquities* |
| Barn. | Letter of Barnabas |
| CD | Covenant of Damascus = Damascus Document |
| *CH* | Eusebius, *Church History* |
| 1 Clem. | First Letter of Clement |
| 2 Clem. | Second Letter of Clement |
| Col. | Colossians |
| 1 Cor. | First Letter to the Corinthians |
| 2 Cor. | Second Letter to the Corinthians |
| *Dial.* | Justin, *Dialogue with the Jew Trypho* |
| Did. | Didache |
| DioCass. | Dio Cassius |
| Deut. | Deuteronomy |
| Eph. | Ephesians |
| *Ep.mor.* | Seneca, *Epistulae morales* |
| EvEb. | Gospel of the Ebionites |
| EvNaz. | Gospel of the Nazarenes |
| Ezek. | Ezekiel |
| Gal. | Galatians |
| Heb. | Letter to the Hebrews |
| Hos. | Hosea |
| IgnEph. | Ignatius of Antioch, To the Ephesians |
| IgnMagn. | Ignatius of Antioch, To the Magnesians |
| IgnPhilad. | Ignatius of Antioch, To the Philadelphians |

| | |
|---|---|
| IgnSm. | Ignatius of Antioch, To the Smyrnaeans |
| Isa. | Isaiah |
| Jer. | Jeremiah |
| John | Gospel of John |
| 1 John | First Letter of John |
| 2 John | Second Letter of John |
| 3 John | Third Letter of John |
| Jude | Letter of Jude |
| Lev. | Leviticus |
| Luke | Gospel of Luke |
| Mark | Gospel of Mark |
| Matt. | Gospel of Matthew |
| par. | with a parallel tradition in another gospel |
| Phil. | Letter to the Philippians |
| Prov. | Proverbs |
| Ps(s). | Psalm(s) |
| 1QH | Qumran Hodayoth (Cave 1) |
| Q | Logia source |
| Rev. | Revelation = The Apocalypse of John |
| Rom. | Letter to the Romans |
| 1 Thess. | First Letter to the Thessalonians |
| 2 Thess. | Second Letter to the Thessalonians |
| 1 Tim. | First Letter to Timothy |
| 2 Tim. | Second Letter to Timothy |
| ThomEv. | Gospel of Thomas |
| *War* | Josephus, *Jewish War* |

# CHAPTER 1

---

# The 'New Testament' and its Literary Forms

The New Testament is a collection of the writings of a small religious subculture in the Roman empire which formed as a result of a new interpretation of the Jewish religion. This new interpretation was prompted around AD 27–30 by the activity of the Jewish charismatic Jesus of Nazareth, who was executed by the Romans as a troublemaker. In the New Testament writings his figure comes to stand alongside that of God. Even now, one challenge in interpreting these writings is to explain how within the monotheistic world of Jewish faith a human being could come to be associated with the one and only God in this way; how as a result this variant of Jewish religion opened up to non-Jews; and why many Jews had to reject it.

The New Testament comprises twenty-seven short writings which were composed between AD 50 and AD 130: four gospels, twenty-one letters, the Acts of the Apostles and the Revelation of John (the Apocalypse). All are written in Greek. When they were written there was as yet no 'New Testament'. The holy scriptures of the Jews in their Greek translation were the Bible of the first Christians; they are called 'Septuagint' (from the Latin word for seventy), after the legendary seventy translators of the Hebrew Bible, the Old Testament. Jews were the first in history to develop the idea of a canon (Greek 'measure and guideline'), i.e. a collection of writings which impressed the content and convictions of a religion on the cultural memory of a community as something holy, in order

1

to prevent the community from ever forgetting them. The first Christians developed their expanded 'canon' on the model of the Jewish canon. Here the Jewish Bible became the 'Old Testament' only to distinguish it from their own 'New Testament'. Both together formed the basis of the new religion that was coming into being, namely the Christian Bible.

The idea of a closed collection of scriptures which as the 'New Testament' completed and surpassed the Old Testament canon had developed by around AD 180; it is to be found in the writings of Irenaeus of Lyons, but there was a dispute until the fourth century over whether certain writings (Hebrews, James, 2 Peter, 2/3 John, Jude, Revelation) formed part of it. Alongside the canonical writings there was a rich primitive Christian literature which was not incorporated into the canon. There were 'apocryphal' gospels (from the Greek *apokrypha* = hidden), the most significant of which is the Gospel of Thomas, discovered in 1945. And there were also the so-called 'apostolic fathers', writings which rightly or wrongly were attributed to 'disciples of the apostles': the letters of Ignatius of Antioch, the two letters of Clement and the letter of Barnabas, the Shepherd of Hermas, and the 'Teaching of the Apostles' or the 'Didache' (= Greek 'doctrine'). A history of the origin of the New Testament must explain why these and other writings were not included in the canon.

A first attempt to understand the 'New Testament' as literature can begin either from the title of the whole collection of books or from the literary forms of the writings brought together in it.

The title 'New Testament' derives from the Hebrew term 'new covenant' and appears for the first time as a promise in the book of the prophet Jeremiah (31.31–34): one day God will no longer write his commandments on stone but in the hearts of the Israelites, so that no human teacher has to hand them on. People will automatically be guided by them, for God will give them a new heart (cf. Jer. 24.7; Ezek. 11.19; 36.26). This new relationship with God was regarded as the 'new covenant' which God will make with Israel. Inspired by this vision, in the second century BC, in reaction to tendencies towards Hellenization in Judaism, some Jews founded a 'new covenant in the land of Damascus' (CD 6.19; 8.21; 20.12) – a group which later resulted in the Essenes. Its founder, the Teacher of Righteousness, gave the group its final form. He was probably a high priest forced out of office in the middle of the second century BC, who created a 'divine covenant' from already existing reform groups. He also called the group 'my covenant' (1QH V, 23). This refers to the tremendous claim to revelation which he made: the 'holy scriptures' were now being fulfilled in him, if they were understood in the way that had been revealed to him. However, the term 'new covenant' did not become established among the Essenes. They usually called their community the 'covenant of grace', the 'eternal covenant' or the 'covenant of eternal fellowship'. They wanted to realize God's age-old covenant with Israel. In antiquity the term 'new' had negative connotations. There was a widespread conviction that the old was better, and the 'new' often an error.

Here the first Christians judged differently: they set their new covenant over against the old covenant (2 Cor. 3.14) and understood it as the completion of the old. What was the new feature? If we follow the terminology of the 'new covenant' we come upon the three forms of expression of any religion: ethic, rite and myth. Far-reaching changes came about in all of these.

The 'new covenant' aims at a new *ethic*. Paul introduces his contrast between the old covenant and the new with words from the promise of Jeremiah: Christians are a letter, 'written not with ink but with the Spirit of the living God, not on tablets of stone but on tablets of human hearts' (2 Cor. 3.3). He has a clear vision of ethical commandments which no longer guide people from outside, but from within, by the spirit which fundamentally renews them. In fact primitive Christianity (like Hellenistic Judaism generally) combined the traditional Jewish ethic of commandments with a Hellenistic ethic of insights. Paul wants to 'prove what is the will of God' (Rom. 12.2) and thus combine the Socratic requirement to examine everything with the affirmation of God's commandments. Philo of Alexandria (first half of the first century AD) was convinced that a universally valid 'law of nature' had been revealed on Sinai, which had also found an echo in the Greek philosophers and into which reason had insights. The Christians hoped that the Spirit of God would make God's commandments evident to them.

Along with the new ethic went a new *rite*: the notion of the 'new covenant' governed the celebration of the eucharist, with the words, 'This cup is the new covenant in my blood. Do this, as often as you drink from it, in remembrance of me' (1 Cor. 11.23–25). What was new here? The eucharist replaced the bloody sacrifices which people from primitive times had seen as the centre of any religion. Their place was taken by bread and wine – and the remembrance of a death interpreted as a form of sacrifice which at that time had long been superseded: human sacrifice. Whereas the bloody animal sacrifice had been abolished and replaced by a harmless meal, the religious imagination was captured by the interpretation of a violent execution. But this one particular human sacrifice was regarded as the end of all bloody sacrifices (this is explained at length in the letter to the Hebrews). This change, too, belongs in a wider context. In Judaism a service of the word which did not involve sacrifice had already developed in the synagogue alongside the sacrificial cult in Jerusalem. The first Christians continued it. They replaced sacrifice by a sacral meal of bread and wine. At the same time criticisms of sacrifice could be heard among non-Jews – above all among Neopythagoreans, who regarded all life as interrelated and believed in a reincarnation of dead men and women in animals. Moreover, after the destruction of the temple in AD 70 Jews developed a form of worship without sacrifice in which the study of the laws of sacrifice and doing good replaced the bloody sacrifices.

Finally, the term 'new covenant' refers to the *myth* of the first Christians. Here the term 'myth' has the neutral meaning of the 'basic narrative of a religion' which is the basis of rite and ethics. This does not indicate anything about its truth value. As 'New Testament', the term 'new covenant' became established as a designation for the collection of writings that contained this narrative. A conceptual shift between the

Hebrew *b{e}rit* (covenant, dispensation) and the Greek *diatheke* (dispensation, testament) facilitated this. The 'covenant' (*b{e}rit*) originally denoted a relationship of obligation between God and his people like that between king and vassal. The translation of *b{e}rit* (covenant) by *diatheke* made it possible to understand this 'covenant' also as a 'testament' – the will of a dying man. For in Greek *diatheke* can mean 'testament'. But this conceptual shift does not explain everything. The fact that in the writings of the New Testament the narrative of Jesus was brought into the centre was far more decisive. This narrative took the place occupied in other religions by myth. But whereas as a rule the myth took place in a grey prehistory when the world was created and took its due form, in primitive Christianity the myth told of a historical figure in the midst of time. Here, too, the first Christians continued what Jews had begun: in the sacred writings of the Jews historical narratives had become the fundamental narrative of a religion. Here already the myth of primeval time was continued down to the present by narratives – and this involuntarily gave the present the aura of myth.

So the term 'New Testament' points to a new ethic, a new rite and a new myth (attested in the primitive Christian writings). In what follows these writings will have a central place. A second stage in approaching them is to look at their genres. The language of literary forms often reveals the intentions of a group far more unerringly than what is actually said. Here, too, it is illuminating to look at the Teacher of Righteousness, since with his claim to revelation he is most closely comparable to Jesus.

Not even the name of the Teacher of Righteousness has come down to us. But we do have some of his writings: psalms which sing of the nothingness of human beings and their predetermination to salvation through God's election, and a letter to the high priest in office in which he discusses the ritual differences that have led to the separation of him and his followers from the temple. Despite the existence of such original writings, no second part of the canon, in which the writings of the Teacher of Righteousness were added to the

Bible, came into being among the Essenes. Only the holy scriptures of Judaism were regarded as the canon. But because the Essenes (and other Jews) had a great longing for new revelations, they supplemented them by deutero-canonical writings, which derived their authority from the canonical writings of the 'Old Testament'.

- Among the Essenes the Old Testament story was retold – for example, large parts of Genesis in the 'Genesis Apocryphon'. Later, works of this kind certainly came into being among the first Christians (for example, parts of the 'Ascension of Isaiah'), but they are absent from their canon. The Christians did not want to re-tell old history but make known a new history.

- The Essenes also read (and produced) revelatory writings which were attributed to great figures of the Old Testament like Enoch, Abraham or Ezra. In these writings human beings were transported to heaven, there to learn secrets which would allegedly be made known only in the present. Here new insights were offered as age-old revelations. They received their authority from Old Testament figures. The New Testament contains only one revelatory writing of this kind, the Apocalypse (or Revelation) of John. But this is attributed to a contemporary prophet who was known to the readers of the book, John of Patmos. It seeks to be living prophecy for the present and does not derive its authority from age-old seers and revealers.

- Finally, the Essenes produced writings containing legal regulations for the community. The 'Temple Scroll' sets out to be a new revelation received by Moses on Sinai, in which God himself speaks in the first person. It probably aimed to become the 'sixth book of Moses'. Similarly, the first Christians created writings which, given their claim, were meant to take their place along-side the Old Testament writings – not, however, as a reformulation of the old revelation of Moses, but as the communication of a new revelation. In them Jesus appears as a new Moses and says, 'You have heard that

it was said to the men of old . . . But I say to you . . .'.
(Matt. 5.21–22)

Unlike the Teacher of Righteousness, Jesus did not leave a
single writing; instead, his followers composed writings about
him and made them into a new canon. The source of its
authority is Jesus of Nazareth. As a collection, these writings
have the Old Testament as a model. It was only in dependence
on the Old Testament that the New Testament came into
being. But remarkably this dependence did not affect the two
basic genres of the New Testament. Neither gospels nor
collections of letters have a model in the Old Testament; they
were formed out of the traditions and needs of primitive
Christian communities – in dependence more on formal
models in the non-Jewish world than on Jewish literature.

The gospel is a variant of the ancient 'life', which was
widespread in the non-Jewish world: the gospel is an ancient
*bios* (a better term to use than 'biography'), though a *bios* of
an unusual kind. The oldest gospel, the Gospel of Mark, does
not begin with the birth and childhood of Jesus. And it breaks
off with the discovery of the empty tomb – as if it hesitates to
narrate the story of the Risen Christ on the same level as his
life hitherto. Luke and Matthew are the first to add narratives
about Jesus' childhood and to round off the gospel with
appearances of the Risen Christ. It is striking that nowhere in
the Old Testament do we find a literary genre that is so centred
on a person as the gospels are. The five books of Moses tell
the story of the world and a people – but not the story of
Moses. Philo of Alexandria was the first to write a life of Moses
(among other things for pagan readers). By contrast, lives
were widespread in the non-Jewish world. Thus the very form
of the gospels shows that they stand on the threshold between
Judaism and non-Jewish culture. In them the traditions about
Jesus were organized in a form which has more analogies
outside Judaism than within it. Moreover, the gospel form
puts an individual at the centre of the interpretation of the
world and life – and in a way that is alien to Judaism. A
comparison with the Teacher of Righteousness shows this.
He too was the founder of a new movement in Judaism which

could have become a separate religion had it not perished in
the Jewish war of AD 66–74. He too made a great claim to
revelation. Nevertheless his life was not written down by his
followers. We have original testimonies to him, but know far
less about his life than about Jesus of Nazareth. Although the
concentration of religion on a singular figure was far more
advanced in his case than elsewhere in Judaism, it was not
strong enough to lead to the formation of literature.

The second main form of literature in the New Testament,
the letter, is also illuminating. The letter became established
before the gospel: the authentic letters of Paul, which were
written between AD 50 and AD 56, are older than the canonical
gospels, which were composed between 70 and 110. We
find letters in two collections: the thirteen letters of Paul, which
are addressed to individual communities and persons (the
letter to the Hebrews, which does not mention Paul directly
as its author, is counted as the fourteenth letter of this
collection), and the seven Catholic letters, which are addressed
to all Christians ('catholic' means 'universal'). These comprise
the letter of James, the two letters of Peter, three letters of
John and the letter of Jude. Certainly there are isolated letters
in the Old Testament writings, like Jeremiah's letter to the
exiles in Babylon (Jer. 29), but these letters were not
developed into an independent literary form. So we find no
models in the Old Testament and in Judaism for the New
Testament collections of letters. However, we do find such
models in the non-Jewish world, where the letters of Plato or
the Cynics were circulated. Latin authors like Cicero published
their letters. This again confirms that the language of the New
Testament forms shows that in primitive Christianity we are
on the frontier between Jewish and non-Jewish culture. If we
could derive the improbable concentration of the New
Testament on one person from the dominance of the gospel
form, the letter form tells us something more, for example
about the sociological structure of the new movement: it
existed in a network of small communities extending beyond
the local region. Its letters mostly represent the interventions
of primitive Christian authorities in the life of the communities. In them we detect the concern that Christian faith

should permeate the everyday life of Christians. Primitive Christianity combined an intensity that permeated life with a breadth extending beyond the local region.

The letters bear witness to Jesus in a different way from the gospels. They contain only a few fragments of the tradition about the earthly Jesus of Nazareth. In them Jesus appears as a supernatural being sent from God's pre-existent world who became a man, suffered death and then rose from the dead to be exalted as ruler over all powers. It was not what Jesus taught and said that was important, but what God wanted to do and say through him. This form of reference is often called the kerygmatic proclamation of Christ as distinct from the Jesus tradition ('kerygmatic' means 'proclamatory'). In it Jesus has become very much more a mythical being than in the first three gospels, which are taken together, as synoptic gospels, because of the affinity between them. The fact *that* Jesus was a man and that he was *crucified* is of decisive importance in the letters: here a divine being enters and leaves the human world. Of course there are points of contact between these two forms of reference to Jesus. The crucifixion and resurrection also play a role in the Jesus tradition. And the mythical splendour of the proclamation of Christ also keeps breaking through in the traditions about the earthly Jesus. But anyone can sense the difference by setting side by side two summary formulations of the Jesus tradition and the proclamation of Christ. In Phil. 2.6–11 Paul quotes a hymn in two strophes (it is traditionally known as the 'Philippians hymn'). He probably already found it as a tradition, though we cannot rule out the possibility that he himself composed this primitive Christian poetry:

> He was like God,
> but did not hold on to being like God;
> he emptied himself
> and became like a slave
> and like human beings.
> His life was that of a man;
> he humbled himself
> and was obedient unto death,
>> unto death on the cross.

> Therefore God has exalted him above all
> and given him the name
> which is greater than any name,
> that all in heaven, on earth and under the earth
> should bow their knee to the name of Jesus
> and every mouth confess:
> Jesus Christ is the Lord –
>     to the glory of God, the Father.

We would have to read a whole gospel to find an example of the Jesus tradition. Here, though, a retrospective summary can be a substitute for the whole. In the Gospel of Luke, after the death of Jesus, the disciples on the road to Emmaus meet the risen Christ without recognizing him and report to him the great disappointment of their lives, about Jesus:

> 'He was a prophet, mighty in deed and word before God and all the people. But our high priests and leaders condemned him to death and nailed him to the cross. But we had hoped that he was the one to redeem Israel. Yes, and besides all this, it is now the third day since this happened . . .'. (Luke 24.19ff.)

The Jesus tradition in the synoptic gospels about the words and deeds of Jesus and the Christ proclamation of the action of God in the letters of Paul (or in the pre-Pauline traditions in them) first come together in the Johannine writings (the gospel and the letters): here the earthly Jesus himself becomes the one who proclaims the Christ. He preaches about himself, as Paul preached about him. At the climax of the farewell discourses in the Gospel of John, Jesus sums up his mission like this: 'I came from the Father and have come into the world; again, I am leaving the world and going to the Father' (John 16.28).

But how are we to assess the two 'genres' in the New Testament canon which are represented by only one example of each, the Acts of the Apostles and the Apocalypse of John? How could they come to find a place in the New Testament as the sole representatives of their genres? Both genres have models in the Old Testament canon (or at least in the Jewish literature between the Old Testament and the New Testament), and both have connections with the two basic genres of the New Testament. They found their way into the New Testament canon in the wake of the gospel form (Acts) or the letter form (Apocalypse) respectively.

Acts, written by the author of the Gospel of Luke, is a continuation of the biblical historical writing which is represented in the Old Testament by, for example, the books of Judges and Kings. It is even closer to the history writing of the Hellenistic period, the first two books of Maccabees and the *Jewish Antiquities* of Flavius Josephus (*c.* AD 37–100), in which he narrates the history of the Jews from the creation until his time. At about the same time 'Luke' wrote his history of the first Christians; however, this does not go back into grey prehistory but begins in the most recent present. His prologue (Luke 1.1–4) indicates that when he refers to eyewitnesses and sources and disparages his 'many' predecessors he is working with the claims of a historian of antiquity. By the form of his work alone he indicates that the small group of Christians deserves to be described in a historical work just as much as the great peoples and kings. It is here that the history of the world is decided for him. But despite support from biblical models, the Acts of the Apostles found a place in the canon only in the wake of the Gospel of Luke. It was accepted into the canon as its 'second volume' (Acts 1.1). It describes the penetration of Christianity into the world of old beliefs, dominated by Rome, and sets out to give Christians a place in the Roman empire.

There is also an Old Testament model for the Apocalypse of John: the book of Daniel, which depicts in visions the conflict between the rule of God and the empires of the world. In addition there are apocalyptic revelatory writings from the period after the Old Testament. This sole New Testament example of a genre is also supported by a rich tradition when it depicts the rule of God in conflict with the rule of Rome. And the Apocalypse, too, could find a place in the canon only in the wake of another genre: its external framework is a letter. After a preface it begins like a letter: 'John to the seven churches in the province of Asia, grace be to you . . .' (Rev. 1.4). And at the end it concludes like a letter, with a blessing (Rev. 22.1; cf. Heb. 13.25). The seven letters to the churches are an essential part of the apocalypse (Rev. 2.1 – 3.22). Despite the Old Testament model, the dependence on the letter form is unmistakable. Whereas Acts corresponds in the language of its form to Hellenistic genres, in the Apocalypse we have a literary form rooted in Judaism. In content, too, it is opposed to Acts. Whereas in Acts compromise with the Roman empire seems possible, for the Apocalypse there can only be a fundamental opposition; the Roman empire is a satanic beast from the abyss (Rev. 13).

Thus the language of the literary forms of the New Testament already tells us a good deal about the groups which produced them: they come from Judaism and penetrate the non-Jewish world, whose literary form they often imitate in an independent way. At the centre of their faith stands a single figure, Jesus of Nazareth. They spread all over the Mediterranean area, and engage in intensive communication extending beyond local regions; the extant letter literature is only part of this. They have an ambivalent attitude to the Roman empire.

Because the forms of the two basic genres did not exist in the Old Testament, the new primitive Christian writings could not simply supplement the Old Testament canon. At most the earliest collection of sayings of Jesus (which is no longer extant), the so-called 'logia source', could have joined the other prophetic books as the thirteenth of them. But it is not by chance that the genre of the collection of sayings did not find a place in the canon. It does not show clearly enough what was 'new' about the new movement. However, the ultimate reason for setting apart the Old Testament canon as a separate part of the canon does not lie in the language of the forms of the New Testament but in the fact that this new language of forms had been evoked by a charismatic whose activity was given critical impulses by his own Jewish traditions. The first Christians were well aware that while the Old Testament writings were holy scripture, they were not binding in all points. Not everyone followed their ritual law: Gentile Christians neither had their children circumcised nor observed the regulations about food. Thus with primitive Christianity a movement came into being which showed great loyalty to the Old Testament writings, but at the same time criticized them and dissociated itself from some of their precepts. The first Christians discovered a deep ambivalence – as deep as that between life and death – in the holy scriptures which they venerated as God's revelation. Paul expresses it with the following saying: 'The letter kills, but the spirit gives life' (2 Cor. 3.6). In modern times we have grown accustomed to looking at the most sacred traditions with a critical eye. So we find it difficult to imagine what a great step it was for the first Christians to criticize the old – and to do so in the conviction that they were thus fulfilling its deepest intentions. The key to the historical understanding of this remarkable combination of loyalty to a sacred tradition and innovation is the activity of Jesus of Nazareth.

# CHAPTER 2

# Jesus of Nazareth

Jesus of Nazareth left no writings. Nevertheless the language of the forms of his preaching has found its way into the gospels. We find it here as a unique combination of poetry in parables, wisdom in sentences and prophecy in promises and threats. In addition he has indirectly helped to stamp the recollection of his activity in brief anecdotal narratives (apophthegms) and miracle stories. Everything that is said by him and about him in the gospels is bathed in a mythical aura, yet it is moulded by a concrete history which fits only into the Jewish world of the first century AD. There is no contradiction here: in those days people lived in mythical categories. So did the historical Jesus. He and his followers experienced reality as the arena of supernatural powers, in which God and the devil, angels and demons fought together. For them history in-cluded myth, in so far as myth was alive among them. But what do we know of this Jesus of Nazareth – including his 'mythical' world? What follows can only be a brief sketch.

Jesus came from Galilee. He made his first public appear-ance as a follower of John the Baptist. His baptism must be historical, as the self-accusation that he was a sinner associated with it was a scandal to the first Christians, since from a very early stage they were convinced of his sinlessness (Heb. 4.15). In the Jewish-Christian Gospel of the Nazarenes Jesus initially refuses to have himself baptized (EvNaz. 2). In the Gospel of the Ebionites John the Baptist even kneels before him to be baptized by him (EvEb. 3) And while the Gospel of John has Jesus coming to be baptized laden with sins, they are not his sins, but the sins of the world (John 1.29). A tradition which causes so much trouble to apologists (and which is so widely attested) has a historical nucleus.

If Jesus was a follower of John the Baptist, he shared John's conviction that the end of the world was near and that only radical repentance could save people from the judgment. We also find in Jesus the expectation of an imminent end and a call to repentance (Luke 13.1–9; 15.1ff.), but he did not baptize – at least during the time of his public activity (John 3.22 is retracted in 4.2). In contrast to John the Baptist, this already indicates an indifference to ritual acts and a greater trust in the grace of God. For John the Baptist thought that the axe had already been laid to the roots of the trees (Luke 3.9). So there was no time to attest the authenticity of repentance by actions. Therefore baptism as a symbolic substitute action took their place. Jesus must have seen that the imminent end preached by John was not materializing. John was arrested. Time went on. Jesus probably regarded ongoing time as grace, as an opportunity for repentance and life. For him, the simple fact that the sun rises is a sign of God's goodness (Matt. 5.45). He was convinced that God gave people time to repent, as is shown by the parable of the barren fig tree (Luke 13.6–9).

We can reconstruct the basic features of Jesus' preaching as a consequence of which he became independent of John the Baptist. For we have many traditions about Jesus that are potentially independent of one another: the Gospel of Mark and the logia source (Q), along with the special material in Matthew and Luke, i.e. traditions attested only in one of these gospels. The Gospels of John and Thomas probably also contain independent Jesus traditions. These traditions are always pieces of tradition, each of which could be handed down separately before being written down in the framework of a gospel. To this degree, in each 'pericope' (i.e. in each section and piece of tradition) we possess a potentially independent tradition. The forms, motifs and words that recur in them could have been influenced by the historical Jesus, as

could material which contradicted the tendencies to venerate
him in primitive Christianity and which were therefore only
handed down one by one. We can check the results that we
arrive at here from our growing knowledge of the historical
background of the time. Here I follow two criteria in the
reconstruction of the historical Jesus. (1) According to the
criterion of *plausibility of influence*, whatever can better be
explained as the influence of the historical Jesus than by
other factors is authentic. Accordingly, agreements between
independent traditions and remains of a conflict with primitive Christian faith and life contained in them are above all
historical. (2) According to the criterion of *plausibility of
contact*, whatever can be regarded as an individual phenomenon in the historical context of the time is authentic. For
what could be imagined in the first half of the first century in
Galilee is more a product of Jewish history than a fantasy of
primitive Christianity. All in all, we may say that what can best
explain how a charismatic rooted in Judaism could found a
movement which after his death spread above all among
Gentiles is most likely to be historical in the Jesus tradition.
In my view, we can say the following in this connection.

Like John the Baptist, Jesus appeared with an eschatological
message. He expected the imminent end of the world
('eschaton' = end). He preached the *basileia tou theou*, which
we can translate as both 'kingly rule' of God and 'kingdom of
God'. In his preaching he expresses a consistent monotheism:
the one and only God will ultimately enter into his rule and
win through against the evil powers, the demons in the world
and the sins in human beings. Jesus' contemporaries knew
what he meant. Nowhere does he explain to them what
'kingdom of God' means. But he puts the emphasis in
particular places. (1) In other Jewish texts about the 'kingly
rule' of God, God is always also 'king'. Certainly Jesus
speaks about the 'kingly rule' of God, but not about God as
'king'; he speaks about God as 'father'. God is presented as a
gracious power who establishes himself in the world and with
whom his children have a privileged relationship. The
petition, '*Father*, hallowed be your name. Your *kingdom* come'

(Luke 11.2) is characteristic of him. (2) In other Jewish texts the kingly rule of God lies in the future, but for Jesus it already begins in the present, when he drives out demons (Luke 11.20 par.). It is like a seed that is present now, but in a hidden way; soon it will become visible and ready for the harvest (Mark 4.26–29). (3) In other Jewish texts the kingly rule of God represents liberation from alien Gentile rule, often through a military victory. But for Jesus the aliens and the Gentiles (perhaps together with the diaspora Jews?) are the ones who will stream into the kingly rule of God (Luke 13.29 par.). God's kingly rule does not represent a triumph over the enemies of Israel but hope for the lost and the disadvantaged in Israel. In it, aliens and foreigners will have priority over the native inhabitants.

Consequently, this preaching is very much more a message of joy and grace than the message of John the Baptist. However, the judgment is not absent. According to Jesus, too, not all will enter the kingdom of God: 'Amen I say to you, whoever does not receive the kingdom of God like a child shall not enter it' (Mark 10.15). The judgment will separate people who are closely associated: 'I tell you, in that night there will be two men in one bed; one will be taken and the other left. There will be two women grinding together; one will be taken and the other left' (Luke 17.34–35).

Jesus was sure about the dawn of the kingdom of God because he found that he had a capacity for miraculous healings in the present. He was a charismatic healer, of the kind that we find in many cultures (and also in the modern world). People told of his miracles during his lifetime and often exaggerated them. The miracles have a historical nucleus: they are attested in narrative and sayings traditions (cf. Luke 7.18–23; 10.13; 11.20), and at that time not all charismatics were credited with them. We do not hear of either the Teacher of Righteousness or John the Baptist performing miracles (cf. John 10.41). They pile up in a quite extraordinary way in the Jesus tradition. However, it is not this that makes his miracles special but the fact that he fits them into the world of his convictions. They spread the certainty that salvation is coming now. It is already dawning. Evil is fleeing.

Jesus saw the power to overcome evil in people themselves. The promise 'Your faith has helped you' (Mark 5.34, etc.) could go back to the historical Jesus.

Jesus used the language of the forms of prophecy and wisdom to proclaim his message of the kingdom of God. Even if we are uncertain whether he spoke a particular saying in one way and not another, we are very well informed about the forms of the language he used. Jesus spoke in beatitudes, in which he praised the unfortunate because in the present their situation would take a turn for the better: 'Blessed are you poor, for yours is the kingdom of God' (Luke 6.20). And he pronounced woes: 'Woe to you teachers of the law! You have taken away the key (the door) to knowledge . . .' (Luke 11.52).

Jesus coined sayings in the first person in which he speaks of his mission with the phrase 'I have come . . .' (Luke 12.49–50, 51; 7.34; Mark 2.17). Some scholars have wanted to interpret these sayings as a retrospect on his life by primitive Christian prophets. But Josephus, too, could use these terms of himself on his emergence as a prophet (*War* 3, 400). We can be even more confident that Jesus used such language. The antitheses in the Sermon on the Mount are also sayings in the first person. Only in the case of the first two does the antithetical form go back to Jesus; the rest have been shaped on that model. In them Jesus sets his 'But I say to you' over against Moses, not to contradict Moses' prohibition of killing and adultery but to develop the motif in order to expose the forbidden actions that happen within people, in their anger and their desires (Matt. 5.21–22; 5.27–28). He does not say 'You shall not be angry,' or 'You shall not have sexual desires.' He simply says that those who are angry are guilty, and those who lust after someone else's wife have committed adultery. This is also focused on recognizing one's own imperfection – just as wisdom sayings are often primarily focused on knowledge.

The same goes for pointed little sentences in which for example Jesus indicates his scepticism about the distinction between 'clean and unclean'. Nothing that enters a person from outside makes him unclean, but only what comes out of him (Mark 7.15). He relativizes the sabbath in a similar way:

'The sabbath was made for man, not man for the sabbath' (Matt. 2.27). Ritual requirements are less important for him than ethical requirements, which he sums up in the twofold commandment to love (Mark 12.28–34). But he did not repudiate ritual behaviour.

He also formulated concrete admonitions – often with a provocative focus: a blow on the cheek should be countered with demonstrative defencelessness and the other cheek should be offered (Luke 6.29) – in the hope of breaking the cycle of violence by 'paradoxical intervention'. A follower who wants to bury his father is told, 'Let the dead bury their dead!' (Luke 9.60). Family piety is to be secondary to the bond with him. On the other hand he calls for love of the enemy (Luke 6.27). Normally people are loyal to kinsfolk and aggressive to outsiders. For Jesus it is the other way round: he expects a break with the family, indeed even the hatred of the closest members of the family (Luke 14.26), but wants to extend love to aliens, enemies and outsiders (Luke 10.30–35; 6.27; 7.36–50).

The extension of love is grounded in God's goodness: just as God makes his sun rise on both the evil and the good and rain fall on both the just and the unjust, so men and women are to overcome the opposition of friend and foe and love their enemies (Matt. 5.44–47). He presented this image of God, in which the gracious side of the Jewish understanding of God shines out, to his hearers in parables, whether by painting pictures which made typical processes in the world like the seed growing by itself transparent to God and human beings, or by relating extraordinary events as the image of the extraordinary character of God's grace. Day labourers are paid the same for different periods of work (Matt. 20.1–16) and a 'wastrel son' is given preferential treatment (Luke 15.11–32). His parables are the earliest examples of the Jewish parable literature, preserved for us in rabbinical writings, which flourished at that time. They are glittering pearls of Jewish poetry. Only the parables of a Jewish parable writer from modern times, Franz Kafka, stand on the same level. Their great theme is human responsibility before God and God's surprising grace, which obligates people to one another.

Those who have received lower wages than others should not grumble (Matt. 20.15). Those who have had a debt remitted by God should remit the debts of others (Matt. 18.23–25). Even those who bend the law in doing this have God on their side (Luke 16.1–8). Even a notorious good-for-nothing should be given a chance – the grumbling of his model older brother puts that brother in the wrong (Luke 15.11–32).

Jesus spread his message in parabolic actions of the kind familiar to us from the prophets of Israel as well as in parables. He chose twelve men from the people for the twelve tribes (Mark 3.14ff.) as the future government of Israel (Matt. 19.28 par.). This was a protest against the contemporary authorities, both Jewish and Roman. Jesus celebrated feasts with 'toll collectors and sinners' in order to depict God's quest for the lost (Luke 7.34; Mark 2.15ff.). He sent out his disciples in demonstrative poverty and asceticism to call on people to repent (Mark 6.6bff.; Luke 10.2ff.). Sending them out like this is hardly a projection back from the period after Easter. For the disciples do not proclaim Jesus but the kingdom of God; they do not call for baptism but for repentance. Their equipment is even sparser than that of the itinerant Cynic philosophers, who took a bag and a staff with them on their way; consequently this strictness was soon toned down: Mark allows them at least a staff and shoes (Mark 6.8–9; Matt. 10.10 differs). At the end of his life Jesus entered Jerusalem on an ass, accompanied by his followers, in a 'counter demonstration' to the marching in of Roman cohorts at the great festivals (Mark 11.1–11). He incurred the opposition of the Jewish temple aristocracy with a symbolic 'cleansing of the temple' (Mark 11.15–18), in which he stripped the temple of its credentials, especially as in parallel to this he announced the destruction of the temple and promised a new temple which would be built by God himself (Mark 14.58). These two symbolic actions brought the conflict in Jerusalem to a head: the entry into Jerusalem heightened the conflict with the political powers, the cleansing of the temple the conflict with the religious powers. Because of these conflicts which he provoked, Jesus probably reckoned with the possibility of a violent death, though he may also have hoped to the last that 'this cup' would pass him by (Mark 14.35–36). He celebrated a last meal in the expectation that he would be celebrating it again with his disciples in the kingdom of God that would soon dawn (Mark 14.25) – either after his death in eternity, or after the dawning of the kingdom of God even before his death. This last meal was understood as his testament: it was his last great symbolic action. However, we can no longer reconstruct it precisely, since the reports have been overlaid by the liturgical practice of the eucharist.

At all events Jesus will have been put to death as a result of a collaboration between the Jewish aristocracy and the Roman provincial administration, just like another prophet called Jesus son of Ananias, a generation later. He prophesied the end of the temple and Jerusalem. The aristocracy arrested him and handed him over to the governor Albinus (*c.* AD 62), who released him as a crazy drop-out (Josephus, *War*, 6, 300ff.). Pilate too could have released Jesus. He is responsible for his execution; there is no doubt about that. Jesus' death on the cross can no more be an invention than his cross. No religious group depicts its redeemer as a criminal who died a dishonourable death on the cross unless it has to. This fact was never doubted in antiquity. Tacitus reports the crucifixion of Jesus in his short note about the Christians and holds Pilate responsible (*Annals*, 15, 44, 3). For him the Christians are a reprehensible people simply because they followed a criminal executed by the Romans. By contrast, the Christians often one-sidedly made the Jewish authorities responsible for Jesus' execution, although the Jews only prepared the accusation before Pilate and did not have the right to impose and inflict the death penalty (John 18.31). We can still recognize that the action against the temple was insufficient grounds for a convincing accusation to the Roman governor; however, the charge of being a messianic royal pretender who wanted to seize power in Palestine was. Jesus' attitude to the temple is mentioned only in the hearing before the Sanhedrin, but it is not sufficient for further proceedings against him. Therefore his accusers pick on the expectation that he is the messiah (Mark 14.55ff. par.). This messiahship of Jesus then plays a role only before the Roman governor. A Roman prefect had to intervene here, once there was a fear that such a claim could provoke political resistance and unrest. An inscription at the crucifixion tells us that Jesus was in fact executed as 'king of the Jews' (Mark 15.26), i.e. as a messianic pretender. Jesus hardly understood himself as a messianic king who would free the land from foreigners, but he did not distance himself before Pilate from the expectation that he was the messiah. For nowhere did the first Christians show themselves perplexed that their master no longer believed in his mission at the end of his life.

Then whom did Jesus understand himself to be? Perhaps he did not attach very much important to a precise notion of who he was. His proclamation was theocentric. God's rule, not his own, was at its centre. He was certainly convinced that he was more than the last Jewish prophet before the dawn of the kingdom of God. John the Baptist had that role. But if John himself was 'more than a prophet' (Luke 7.26), Jesus must have surpassed him. This all-surpassing 'more' can be described like this: Jesus not only announced the kingdom, but brought it in his person. His contemporaries – friends and opponents – therefore hoped or supposed that he was the messiah, the future ruler of Israel. Peter wants to proclaim him as messiah, but in the present version of the story Jesus is evasive about this (Mark 8.27–30). Probably the historical Jesus was in fact cautious about any popular messianic expectation. He was concerned not about 'his kingdom' but about God's kingdom. Possibly he spoke of himself (or a third figure?) using the enigmatic expression 'Son of Man'. This means either 'the man' or 'a man', or is a periphrasis for 'I'. However, there is controversy over this last interpretation. At all events, in primitive Christianity this expression 'Son of Man' was so characteristic of Jesus that (with the exception of Acts 7.56; Rev. 1.13; 14.14) it occurs only in sayings of Jesus. Perhaps in fact Jesus simply wanted to be 'the man' who embodies God's kingdom. Perhaps he spoke of 'the man' in such an emphatic way that he bestowed messianic dignity on this title for all people at all times.

The expectations that he had evoked among his followers were shattered by his crucifixion. His followers had gone up to Jerusalem in the hope that the kingdom of God would break in (Luke 19.11). When after his death they recognized Jesus in visions as being alive, they were convinced that this was the realization of the kingdom of God which they had expected. The kingdom was being realized here and now, but not in the form that they had expected: for them it was not God but Jesus who came into the centre of this kingdom. Thus on the basis of the Easter appearances the theocentricity of the preaching of Jesus became the christocentricity of the preaching about Jesus.

On the basis of the Easter appearances one could understand the exaltation of the crucified Jesus as a break with strict monotheism. And yet it was only a repetition of the dynamic that produced the breakthrough of monotheism during the exile in the sixth century BC. According to the logic of the ancient Near East, with the destruction of Jerusalem in 586 BC and the deportation of the leading class to Babylon Israel and its God had been defeated. The God of the Babylonians had proved to be the stronger God. Israel compensated for the defeat on earth by proclaiming at the moment of the earthly defeat the victory of its God in heaven over all other gods: YHWH the God of Israel was in reality the only God, who stood behind all that had happened. He had made use of the world powers to punish Israel. Even the catastrophe of the destruction of Jerusalem and the exile was his will. The other gods did not exist. The same dynamic repeated itself 600 years later at the origin of Christian faith: the one who had come to grief and had been crucified on earth was exalted to be Lord over all powers and authorities. The greater his failure on earth, the more powerfully his victory in heaven was proclaimed – also as a victory over the powers and authorities who had put him to death (cf. 1 Cor. 2.8; 15.24ff.). The exaltation of the crucified Christ over all the powers was ultimately to serve to establish the rule of the one and only God. It too was focused on a consistent monotheism. Therefore Paul says of the Risen Christ: 'For he (= Christ) must reign until he has put all his enemies under his feet . . . When all things are subjected to him, then the Son himself will also be subjected to him who put all

things under him, that God may be everything to every one'
(1 Cor. 15.25, 28).

Although Jesus did not write a single line, he did make a
decisive contribution to the origin of the New Testament –
not only through the language of the forms that he used,
which have been preserved in the gospels, or simply by virtue
of the fact that he stands at the centre of all the New Testament
writings, but as a result of his awareness of ushering in a
turning point in history in which the relationship between
God, the world and human beings is fundamentally changed.
Because in this awareness he took a step beyond history
hitherto, the writings which he evoked were not just understood as an extension of the Old Testament and subordinate
to it, but were set over against it as the 'New Testament'.
However, this involved a long process. The first attempts to
formulate the tradition about him in writing could still be
understood as a further prophetic book alongside the Old
Testament prophets and to that degree be counted as part of
the Old Testament.

# CHAPTER 3

# The Jesus Tradition in the First Generations: The Logia Source and the Oral Tradition of Jesus

In the period after Easter the way to the New Testament and its two basic forms of gospel and letter leads in two directions in primitive Christianity: on the one hand through the mission to Israel and on the other through the mission to the Gentiles. Both meet in the so-called 'Apostolic Council' in Jerusalem (*c.* AD 46/48). Here the mission to Israel is represented by Peter, John and James the brother of the Lord and the mission to the Gentiles by Paul and Barnabas (cf. Gal. 2.1–10). Paul's mission to the Gentiles is the place where the New Testament letter literature came into being. Paul fashioned it there in the first generation. It is natural to look in the mission to Israel for a line of development which leads to the gospel as the second basic form of the New Testament. However, here we can expect only the prehistory of this form, since the gospels themselves were not written until the second and third generation, after AD 70. Why they came into being only after the letters, although Jesus was far more important than Paul for primitive Christian faith, is a riddle.

Scholarship has been able to shed light on this riddle. It has been able to fill a gap between Jesus and the gospel literature – by the reconstruction of a logia source in which the Jesus tradition was collected at a relatively early stage, and by demonstrating oral traditions which were in circulation a long time before (and alongside) the first written collections of sayings of Jesus. We can make relatively reliable statements about the written logia source; that is more difficult in the case of the oral traditions. Be this as it may, in the sphere of the mission to Israel – at the same time as the composition of the letters of Paul – there was an early literary production: the logia source. With it, in the first generation of the first Christians we come upon the line of development for which we are looking, and which leads us to the gospels in the second generation.

### The sources of the gospels: the synoptic question

The 'logia source' is a collection of sayings of Jesus which can be inferred from the gospels of Matthew and Luke. This prior form of a 'gospel' is the darling of scholars. It owes its existence, about which the tradition of the church is silent, solely to their acute perception. It was discovered within the framework of a solution to the so-called 'synoptic question' (i.e. the question of the literary relationship between the three gospels of Matthew, Mark and Luke). These three gospels are called 'synoptic' (literally: capable of being looked at together), because they are closely connected and can be printed side by side in three columns in a 'synopsis'.

Scholars had long noted that the first three gospels are related in style and content and are clearly distinct from the Gospel of John, forming a threefold tradition. However, there was a debate about how this relationship was to be explained. Were the various gospels based on one primal gospel (G. E. Lessing)? Did they reproduce the same oral tradition independently of one another (J. G. Herder)? Or were they based on small collections of narratives (F. D. E. Schleiermacher)? All possibilities were explored and in the nineteenth century the view became established that the explanation of the relationship between the first three gospels was that they used one another. Here the most probable theory proved to be the 'two-source theory', i.e. the assumption that Matthew and Luke used two sources: the Gospel of Mark, which we still have today, and a sayings source which can only be reconstructed (known by the letter Q, which stands for the German *Quelle*, source). In addition both gospels use special material (Matt[s] and Luke[s]), available to them in oral or written form. The two-source theory is usually presented in the following scheme. In this and in the scheme on page 32, the asterisk denotes versions which have not been preserved but are only postulated:

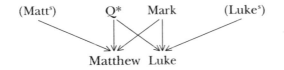

$$(Matt^s) \qquad Q^* \qquad Mark \qquad (Luke^s)$$

Matthew Luke

The two-source theory made the Gospel of Mark, which hitherto had led a shadowy existence in the history of the church and of theology, the most interesting gospel, because it was the earliest. The priority of Mark was inferred from the presence of the substance of Mark (with slight exceptions) in the Gospels of Matthew and Luke and from three observations which can be made in a comparison of the synoptic gospels:

1. Where Matthew and Luke correspond with Mark, they also correspond with each other. Where they do not correspond with Mark, they also diverge from each other. Thus the Gospel of Mark begins with the baptism of Jesus. We hear nothing of Jesus' childhood. Matthew and Luke add accounts of Jesus' birth and infancy, but deviate from one another in so doing: according to Matthew, Jesus comes from Bethlehem; according to Luke he comes from Nazareth. According to Matthew his family are political refugees escaping to Egypt from a massacre of babies in Bethlehem; according to Luke they are model taxpayers who go to Bethlehem on the emperor's orders to register for taxation. We can observe something similar at the end of the gospel: Mark breaks off with the discovery of the empty tomb in Mark

16.8 (a conclusion to Mark which follows in some manuscripts was added at a secondary stage). Again, up to
the story of the empty tomb Matthew and Luke are in
relative agreement in their account of the last days of
Jesus, then they diverge from each other: Matthew
knows an appearance to two women, Luke an appearance to two disciples on the way to Emmaus. Matthew
narrates an appearance on a mountain in Galilee, Luke
only appearances in Jerusalem and Judaea. An obvious
explanation is that as long as Matthew and Luke use
the Gospel of Mark as a common source they agree;
when they lack the support of this common source they
also diverge from each other.

2. This is confirmed by the fact that almost all the
   pericopes that we find in all three gospels have the same
   order in Matthew and Luke as they do in Mark. The
   divergences in Matthew can be explained from his
   aim to bring related texts together, like a cycle of
   miracle stories in Matt. 8 – 9. Where, exceptionally, Luke
   deviates in the sequence of pericopes, he wants, for
   example, to create an audience for Jesus' 'Sermon on
   the Plain' by moving the gathering of the crowd behind
   the call of the Twelve (cf. Luke 6.12–16, 17–19).

3. Finally, we find minor and very minor divergences in
   the wording, which can be best explained as changes
   to the text of Mark by Matthew and Luke: according to
   Mark 10.14 Jesus was, for example, 'unwilling' for the
   disciples to turn away people who brought children to
   him. In Matt. 19.14 and Luke 18.16 we hear nothing of
   an annoyed Jesus. Probably his annoyance was deleted
   because it did not fit either the idealizing of the disciples
   or the veneration of the Master (who was thought to be
   free of human emotions). We have a plausible explanation for the deletion of the motif but not for its addition.
   This test – interpreting deviations as possible changes –
   must of course be applied at many points. Time and
   again it has led to the result that the synoptic gospels
   can be understood better if we assume that Matthew

and Luke used Mark as a basis and occasionally altered the text and its order than if we reckon with other relationships of dependence.

Alongside the 'threefold tradition' there is also a series of 'twofold traditions' in Matthew and Luke in which they agree against Mark. Here, too, agreements and deviations in order and wording can best be explained by the assumption of a common source (= Q). As most of this material which has been handed down twice consists of sayings (or 'logia') of Jesus, this source is called the 'logia source'. Its existence alongside Mark is confirmed by the presence of occasional overlaps between the Mark and the Q material which are recognized as doublets, i.e. as one evangelist reproducing the same tradition twice, once according to Mark and once according to Q. Thus in the Gospel of Luke we find that disciples are sent out twice: first twelve disciples are sent out (Luke 9.1–6), following Mark 6.6–13; then seventy disciples are sent out, following Q (Luke 10.1–12). A first eschatological discourse of Jesus in Luke comes from Q (Luke 17.22–37); a second, more extended, one from Mark 13 (Luke 21.5–36). Finally, there is an impressive statistical argument for the existence of the logia source: where Matthew and Luke reproduce Mark, their common source, which we can check, the verbal agreement between them is 56%. Where we conjecture the source Q, which no longer exists, the figure is as high as 71%. In other words, statistically speaking the argument for the existence of Q is stronger than that for the existence of Mark. If we have to conclude from a 56% verbal agreement that there was a source which exists beyond doubt (the Gospel of Mark) – how much more may we conclude from the 71% agreement that there was a source Q which now no longer exists!

Finally, alongside the threefold tradition in Matthew, Mark and Luke and the twofold tradition in Matthew and Luke there is special material which occurs only in Matthew and Luke respectively (Matt[s] or Luke[s]). It includes well-known pieces of tradition: in Matthew the first antitheses (Matt. 5.21–22, 27–28) and the parables of the 'ungrateful servant'

(18.23–35) and the workers in the vineyard (20.1–16); in Luke the parables of the good Samaritan (Luke 10.30–37), the prodigal son (Luke 15.11–32) and the Pharisee and the publican (Luke 18.9–14). Certainly there is something of a uniform tendency in the special material in each case. The special material in Matthew strikingly has a Jewish-Christian stamp. Jesus does not want to do away with the law and the prophets, but to fulfil them (Matt. 5.17). In Luke there is an impressive picture of the humane Jesus, who turns to sinners and outsiders (Luke 7.36–50). But it is impossible to postulate a written source for each of these traditions of special material. They could be historically related streams of tradition which reached the Gospels of Matthew and Luke in oral form.

Of course there are further differences within the two-source theory. Thus there is a dispute as to whether the two gospels Matthew and Luke used Mark in its present form or in a prior or revised form of the present gospel. In the former case the two long gospels are assumed to depend on an Ur-Mark; in the latter on a Deutero-Mark. These variations on the two-source theory can be depicted by the following scheme:

| Ur-Mark hypothesis | Deutero-Mark hypothesis |
|---|---|
| Ur-Mark* | Mark |
| Mark | Deutero-Mark |
| Matthew          Luke | Matthew          Luke |

The same goes for the logia source Q, which was possibly used by Matthew and Luke in different versions. As a sayings collection, it could easily have been expanded by further sayings. Any copyist would certainly have attempted to add sayings of Jesus that were known to him. And of course time and again there are attempts to challenge the two-source theory generally. None so far has become established.

Now one could still mistrust the sharp-sighted recon-struction by modern scholars. So it should be pointed out that when the two-source theory was developed in the nineteenth century, the notes of a primitive Christian bishop Papias of Hierapolis from the beginning of the second century AD (either *c.* 115 or *c.* 140) on two writings about Jesus that he knew played a role. One note concerns the Gospel of Mark, the other a collection of sayings of Jesus attributed to Matthew. His work, an exposition of the sayings of the Lord, has not survived. But the church father Eusebius knew it in the fourth century AD and quotes from it in his *Church History*.

> Mark, having been the interpreter of Peter, wrote accurately, though not in order, all that he recalled of what was either said or done by the Lord. For he neither heard the Lord, nor was he a follower of his, but, at a later date (as I said), of Peter; who used to adapt his instructions to the needs [of the moment], but not with a view to putting together the oracles of the Lord in orderly fashion: so that Mark did no wrong in thus writing some things as he recalled them. For he kept a single aim in view: not to omit anything of what he heard, nor to state anything therein falsely. (*CH* III, 39.14–15)

> So then, Matthew compiled the oracles in the Hebrew language; but everyone interpreted them as he was able. (*CH* III, 39, 16)

If we read the two notes without prejudice, we will think of the Gospel of Mark as an account of Jesus which contains sayings and actions (which indeed is the case in our Gospel of Mark), while the writing attributed to Matthew must be a collection of sayings. Both were known to Papias in Greek, but he knew of an original 'Hebrew' form of each in either oral (Mark) or written (Matthew) form. We can still also interpret Papias' notes to mean that when he was writing these sentences at the beginning of the second century he had only the two earliest sources of the gospel literature in view. He attributed a collection of logia to Matthew, either because he confused it with the Gospel of Matthew or because the collection of logia which he had was in fact regarded as the work of the apostle Matthew. The collection of logia known to Papias could have been the logia source reconstructed by modern scholars. We could then imagine its further history as follows. The author of the Gospel of Matthew used it as a

source. He wanted to disseminate all over the world the
teaching of Jesus contained in it. So he could have presented
his gospel as a second (improved and enlarged) edition of
the writing of Matthew which he had before him. That would
explain why this collection of logia has not survived as an
independent writing. If two writings were circulating in
primitive Christianity under the same name, one of which
was wholly contained in the other, the longer will have
been preferred to the shorter (as the complete writing of
Matthew). What is important for us here is that we possibly
find a reference to a 'collection of logia' at a very early stage
in primitive Christianity.

## Traditions of the itinerant charismatics:
## the logia source

I had to include this explanation in order to get on the track
of a first written summary of the Jesus tradition by means of
the 'synoptic question'. Of course a precise reconstruction of
this source is difficult. We can never be certain whether it
contained only those traditions which Matthew and Luke have
in common (over against Mark). Nevertheless we can give a
positive description of what was in this source. Here Luke has
preserved the order of the sayings of Jesus in Q better than
Matthew, who has often altered it because of his tendency to
systematize. So in what follows Q will be quoted from the
Gospel of Luke.

The logia source begins (like Mark), with John the Baptist's
sermon (3.2–4). Perhaps it narrated the baptism of Jesus and
his nomination as 'Son of God'. For the temptation of Jesus
which follows (4.1–13) is about his proving himself as 'Son of
God'; it comes to a climax in his refusal to kneel before Satan
to receive rule over the world. As a model Jew and monotheist
he knows that one must not worship anyone other than God.
Because Jesus withstands this trial, he can teach convincingly.

1. His teaching begins with a programmatic discourse
   (6.20–49), which Luke has taken over as the 'Sermon
   on the Plain' and Matthew has fashioned into the

Sermon on the Mount. It starts with beatitudes on the poor, the hungry and those who mourn, followed by woes against the rich and the full. The central demands are love of enemy (6.27–28) and the requirement not to judge one another (6.37–38). It ends by emphasizing the responsibility of the listeners: anyone who does this teaching has built his house on rock – and the catastrophes of judgment will not affect him (6.47–49).

2. After the teaching of Jesus, his impact on his contemporaries and their reaction is described. The story of the centurion of Capernaum (which along with the temptation story is one of the few narratives in Q) shows his effect on Gentiles; here he finds recognition (7.1–10). John the Baptist is hesitant about him and asks doubtingly whether he really is the 'coming one' whom John has announced (7.18–23). By contrast 'this generation', i.e. the generation of Jesus' contemporaries, rejects him and John the Baptist with contradictory arguments like capricious children, although they are both messengers of the wisdom of God, who is wooing her children (7.31–35).

3. After the contemporaries and adversaries, a third section deals with the disciples, their discipleship (9.57–62), the way that they are sent out in demonstrative poverty (10.1–16), and their special relationship with God (10.21–24): the revelation of God about his 'son' (here the movement is from God to human beings) applies exclusively to them, and they in turn may respond to God with the Our Father (11.2ff.), a prayer which has been composed for them (here the corresponding movement is from human beings to God). In the mission discourse we find clear references to the circle of those who hand on the logia source: it is a collection of traditions of itinerant charismatics who continued their itinerant life after the death of Jesus in order to spread his teaching further.

4. A short narrative about an exorcism (11.14–15), a third exception in Q, introduces a new section in which Jesus

argues with opponents. He defends himself against their charge that he is in alliance with Satan (11.17–26). The reader of the logia source knows from the temptation story how unjustified this charge is. Jesus also argues with this 'generation' about their demand for a sign (11.29ff.). The section culminates in a counter-attack, in woes against Pharisees and experts in the law (11.39–52). In it Jesus attacks his opponents with a judgment saying in the name of pre-existent wisdom, whose messengers have been rejected time and again. Therefore now the punishment will come upon 'this generation' (11.49–51).

5. A fifth section with varied content can be summed up under the heading 'the life of the disciples in the light of the end' (12.2ff.). It begins with sayings about fear of men and confessing before human authorities: whoever confesses Jesus will be confessed by Jesus as Son of Man in the heavenly judgment (12.8–9). An admonition not to be anxious once again shows the specific background: those who handed down this tradition worried as little about what they would live on as the birds of the air and the lilies of the field; like the later 'mendicant monks' they lived on the gifts of others (12.22–31). But their eccentric form of life is possible only because the end of the world is near: parables about the coming lord call for watchfulness (12.35–48). The time before the end is a time of testing in which people must reckon with conflicts within the family (12.51–53) but must be reconciled with opponents (12.58–59). One last time Jesus woos Jerusalem like a hen her chickens. He appears once again as wisdom, who calls her children to her (13.34–35). Life on the way to the kingdom of God, attested to by the parables of the mustard seed and the leaven (13.18–21), is like the way through a narrow gate: not all will get through (13.22–30).

A little 'apocalypse' – teaching of Jesus about the end of the world – forms the conclusion of the logia source

(17.22–37). It warns against false messianic expectations and announces the appearance of the 'Son of Man' in cosmic dimensions: he will be visible everywhere like a flash of lightning. He will burst into a peaceful time in which people buy and sell, marry and give in marriage – as unpredictably as the flood in the time of Noah or the destruction of Sodom in the time of Lot. Perhaps Q ended with the saying about the disciples as judges over the twelve tribes of Israel: in a new world they will rule over the renewed people of God (22.28–30).

When was this tradition about Jesus first set down in writing? Since the Son of Man is imagined as coming into a deeply peaceful world (17.22–23), whereas in Mark 13 he comes into a world scarred by the catastrophes of war, it will have been written before the Jewish war. Since the crisis over Caligula has perhaps been used in connection with the temptation on the mountain, i.e. the attempt by the emperor Gaius Caligula in 39/40 to transform the temple into a sanctuary of the imperial cult, the date of the origin of Q lies between AD 40 and 65. Q was composed in Palestine (or in adjoining regions in Syria). The individual traditions indicate a Galilean perspective; they know places as small as Chorazin, Bethsaida and Capernaum (10.13–15).

The traditions of itinerant charismatics are collected in this logia source, i.e. the traditions of the disciples of Jesus who did not give up their itinerant life after Easter but travelled through the land as the missionaries of the new renewal movement within Judaism. They could credibly advocate the radical ethic of Jesus, an ethic of homelessness, detachment from the family, criticism of possessions and non-violence, for which I have proposed the term 'itinerant radicalism'. We read about the homelessness of the disciples in Q: 'The foxes have their dens and the birds their nests, but the Son of Man has nowhere to lay his head' (9.58). Criticism of the family is expressed in the words: 'If anyone comes to me and does not despise father and mother, wife and children, brother and sister, indeed even his own life, he cannot be my disciple' (14.26). It is in keeping with this that the burial of one's father should be left to the dead (9.60–61) and that war is inevitable in families (12.51–53). The families of the radical disciples will hardly have been edified by their abandonment by these disciples. Such circles could credibly cultivate an ethic critical of possessions, declare the poor blessed, criticize the rich and live like birds in the open air (6.20ff.; 12.22ff.). Finally, it was possible for them to practise non-violence: those who are soon leaving the place of their defeat can more easily bear a second blow on their cheeks than those who keep meeting their enemies in the same place (6.29). As the sayings of Jesus have the same setting, namely the life of a homeless itinerant preacher, the primitive Christian itinerant charismatics offer some guarantee that they have preserved the spirit of his words. They continue the preaching of Jesus in the framework of his lifestyle. To begin with they were the real instruments of the new movement. In the villages and small towns which they visited, they gathered small groups of sympathizers around them, and lived on the support that these provided. Their existence can be demonstrated for a long time in the area of Syria and Palestine. Itinerant charismatics are presupposed in the Gospel of Matthew and the Didache. There is a satirical description of one of them in the second century by Lucian of Samosata (in the work *De morte Peregrini*); others are caricatured by Celsus, the opponent of Christianity (in Origen, *contra Celsum* VII, 8–9). The latest evidence for them comes in the pseudo-Clementine letters *de Virginitate* in Syria in the third century. But back to the beginnings!

What picture of Jesus lived on in the circle of his first followers? His childhood and his passion had no role in these circles. All the indications are that Q did not contain any passion story. His death was not regarded as a saving death which frees people from sins; rather, he was regarded as one of the prophets who died a martyr's death for their cause (Luke 11.49–51). Even in this early period some sayings put him near to God. In Q Jesus says of himself: 'All things have been delivered to me by my Father; and no one knows who the Son is except the Father, or who the Father is except the Son and any one to whom the Son chooses to reveal him' (10.22). As the messenger of wisdom he brings to earth the decisive teaching on salvation. As Son of Man and future judge he will decide on salvation and damnation (12.8–9). We may certainly ask whether this does not already break the bounds of strict monotheism. Does not Jesus here already take the place of God? However, we should remember that Jews of the time could imagine divine figures alongside God like Wisdom (Prov. 8) and the Logos (Philo), or a figure like the Son of Man who was comparable to the angels (Dan. 7). God could approach human beings through his 'hypostases' or messengers. But it was unthinkable that a human being should claim to be such a divine figure. And the logia source excludes precisely that. In the temptation story it relates how Jesus strictly rejects the worship of any other being alongside God. This would be a satanic temptation. After Jesus has withstood the test as an exemplary monotheist at the beginning of Q, statements may be made about him which put him near to God.

The logia source had successors in the same genre. The Gospel of Thomas is likewise a collection of sayings of Jesus without a passion story. In them Jesus appears as a revealer who brings a redemptive knowledge (= 'gnosis') from heaven: the Gospel of Thomas represents a developed form of such collections of sayings. It not only hands down sayings of Jesus, but offers their true interpretation. It is decisive for salvation. That is said programmatically in the first logion: 'Whoever finds the interpretations of these sayings will not experience death' (1). The interpretation is that the 'kingdom of God' does not denote any external reality but the innermost self of the human being, which comes from heaven but has forgotten its origin. Jesus brings these people the redemptive knowledge which reminds them of their heavenly home:

> Jesus said: 'I took my place in the midst of the world
> and I revealed myself to them in the flesh.
> I found all of them intoxicated;
> I found none of them thirsty.
> And my soul became afflicted;
> for they are blind in their hearts,
> and do not have sight,
> for empty they came into the world,

and empty too they seek to leave the world.
But for the moment they are intoxicated.
When they shake off their wine, then they will repent.'

(ThomEv. 28)

So we may assume that the social background to the Gospel
of Thomas is also an itinerant charismatic movement (cf.
ThomEv. 14), probably in Syria, where the Thomas traditions have their home. The more the primitive Christian
itinerant charismatics came up against repudiation in the
'normal local communities', the more they became open to
radical notions which presupposed a dualism between the
world and God. They found themselves isolated, and understood themselves as the 'solitary' in this world: 'Jesus said:
Blessed are the solitary and the elect, for you will find the
kingdom. For you are from it, and to it you will return'
(ThomEv. 49). However, the tendency towards gnosis
which is becoming visible here is not fully established in the
Gospel of Thomas. Thomas lacks, for example, belief in a
second creator God alongside the true God. But what is
important for us is that before the discovery of the Gospel
of Thomas in 1945 the existence of a logia source could
still be doubted because there was no evidence that such a
genre existed in primitive Christianity. Now this argument
has been refuted.

We can also assume from a comparison between the logia
source and the Gospel of Thomas that a deliberate composition must underlie Q. So far it has not proved possible to
demonstrate a clear structure in the Gospel of Thomas –
except in very rough outline. By contrast, it is possible to trace
the structure of the logia source, especially at the beginning
and at the end. As always in writings with collected material
the order in the middle is rather more open, because here
other traditions are collected which are important to the
author but are more difficult to put in order. But apart
from this composition, it is impossible to demonstrate the
redactional work; above all it is impossible to indicate specific
parts of the final redactional stratum. At most here one can
point to the narrative parts, the temptation story and the

narrative of the centurion of Capernaum, because they are clearly different in form from the sayings traditions.

In genre, the logia source is a prophetic book which has incorporated a large number of wisdom sayings. Like the prophetic books of the Old Testament, it does not narrate the death of the prophet and says only a little about his life. In terms of genre it could have been accepted into the Old Testament canon as a further prophetic book. In Q, as in these prophetic books, authentic sayings of Jesus will have stood alongside sayings of his 'disciples': sayings which often existed as variations on authentic sayings or were formed in analogy to them. But there were also new creations. Thus the revelation saying quoted above, 'All things have been delivered to me by my father . . .' (Luke 10.22), seems like the saying of a primitive Christian prophet spoken in the name of the exalted Christ. In Matt. 28.18 the Risen Christ himself says: 'All power is given to me in heaven and on earth . . .'.

The logia source shows a deep link with Judaism not only in its genre but also in its content. There are no sayings and pericopes which are critical of the law. Certainly Gentiles are depicted as exemplary, but they serve above all to lead Israel to repentance. The logia source also gives a last chance to the Israelites who have rejected Jesus' message. Jesus calls to those who have killed prophets and stoned messengers (in the name of Wisdom): 'You will not see me until you say, "Blessed is he who comes in the name of the Lord"' (Luke 13.35). At the same time Paul knows a comparable hope: at the return of the Lord all Israel will be saved (Rom. 11.26). In my view the hope was alive in the first generation that the division between Jews and Christians would have been overcome at the latest at the parousia of Jesus (his 'coming' as exalted ruler in glory). But exegetes strongly dispute this.

### Traditions of the local communities:
### the passion and the synoptic apocalypse

Not all the traditions about Jesus were collected together in the logia source; only the words which were proclaimed by itinerant charismatics and which legitimated their existence. Alongside them from the beginning there were groups of sympathizers who remained where they lived. The local community in Jerusalem was the most significant of these – not only as the 'home port' of many itinerant charismatics, but also as the place of the last days of Jesus. It seems likely that memories of his passion were handed down in this community.

The story of the passion occupies a special place in the Jesus tradition. As a rule stories about Jesus consist of small, well-rounded units. But in the passion story there is a consecutive narrative thread which links several units, whether this is a shorter report of the arrest, interrogation, condemnation and crucifixion of Jesus beginning in Mark 14.43ff. or a longer report which begins as early as Mark 14.1ff. and in addition narrates Jesus' parting from his disciples with the anointing, the last supper and the night in Gethsemane. At all events there is a striking agreement between the synoptic gospels and the Gospel of John in the passion story. One explanation would be that they depend on a common passion story.

'Indications of familiarity', i.e. references in the text which presuppose an improbable familiarity with the persons and places mentioned in it, suggest an early date for the passion story. On the way to the execution Simon of Cyrene is compelled to carry Jesus' cross (Mark 15.21). He is introduced as 'the father of Alexander and Rufus', who are evidently known to those to whom the passion story is addressed – probably as members of the Jerusalem community in which this story was told. At the arrest, two persons remain anonymous: a follower of Jesus who wounds with his sword a member of the squad that is arresting Jesus (Mark 14.47) and another who just manages to escape naked after a hand-to-hand fight (Mark 14.51–52). Otherwise the figures in the passion story are seldom anonymous. In the case of these two figures we could have a protective anonymity: as long as members of the squad which arrested Jesus were still alive, it was inopportune to give the names of the two followers of Jesus who had resisted arrest. So we can reckon that the passion narrative was shaped in Jerusalem in the 40s and 50s. Its absence from the logia source would be understandable if this was being written down around the same time in north Palestine or adjacent Syria.

The passion story is not just concerned to report events, but to cope with them by interpreting them. The disciples had to try to find a meaning in the arrest of Jesus. They told how Jesus went to his death willingly and with his eyes open. He knew that 'the hour is come; now the Son of Man is delivered over to sinners' (Mark 14.41; cf. 14.21). They described his suffering with words from the psalms which spoke of the righteous sufferer who remains faithful to God in all the attacks upon him (Pss. 22; 41; 69). Thus Jesus dies with the words of Ps. 22.2 on his lips: 'My God, my God, why have you forsaken me?' (Mark 15.34). The description of the suffering of Jesus in the language of the psalms shows that the narrators rediscovered their own lives in him. They had become accustomed to identify with the role of the first person speaking in the psalms and to pray the psalms as their lament and their petition. Here they saw Jesus in their role – forsaken by God and fellow human beings.

A second tradition points to southern Palestine. It, too, does not consist of individual pericopes. This is the 'synoptic apocalypse' in Mark 13, in which Mark has worked over an earlier tradition. It prophesies the end time in three phases. First come wars and earthquakes as 'birth pangs' of the new world. They must have been so terrible that some thought that this 'beginning of the woes' was the end. But evidently these crises proved to be woes; in other words the world had gone on (Mark 13.8). Then follows an event which is described enigmatically as 'abomination of desolation' (13.14ff.). Something blasphemous will stand where it should not and will spark off great 'distress' (13.19). The closing phase consists in the appearance of the Son of Man to rescue the elect (13.24ff.). In the middle of this text, people in Judaea are addressed: 'But when you see the desolating sacrilege set up where it ought not to be (let the reader understand), then let those who are in Judaea flee to the mountains' (Mark 13.14). Has Mark taken up a prophecy from the Jewish war here? Or is it a prophecy from the Caligula crisis of 39/40? At that time a statue of the emperor was being made in Phoenicia which was to have been introduced into the temple forcibly by Roman troops. This could have been the 'abomination of desolation'. As soon as it was transported into the 'holy land' or set up in the temple – where it ought not to be – the great eschatological crisis and the end of the world would come. In that case this prophecy could date from the years 39/40 and could look back on the war between Galilee and the Nabataeans which took place in 35/36 as the 'beginning of the woes'. This war was a consequence of the baneful marriage policy of Herod Antipas, which John the Baptist had sharply criticized. The Jewish people had therefore seen the downfall of Herod Antipas as confirmation of John's message – and some certainly also saw it as confirmation of the imminent end which he proclaimed. If God avenges the death of his prophet, he will also intervene soon to fulfil that prophet's message of an imminent end to the world. But despite this the end did not come. In that case the synoptic apocalypse would be a text written as early as 39/40. It is most likely to have been handed down in local communities in Judaea, probably in Jerusalem itself, which had been most affected by the Caligula crisis.

We cannot exclude the possibility that people also collected further traditions about Jesus in the local communities which were gradually forming. Time and again it is conjectured that Mark worked over small collections of anecdotal narratives about Jesus in Mark 2.1 – 3.6 or a small collection of parables of growth in Mark 4.1ff. But by the nature of things that is difficult to demonstrate. At all events, itinerant charismatics were not the only ones who handed down traditions about Jesus. At any rate, these traditions tended to be written down more in local communities. And in addition to that there were also traditions about Jesus which circulated throughout the people.

### Popular traditions: the miracle stories

When the gospels report Jesus' miracles, they often add that rumours of them spread throughout the land (Mark 1.28;

5.20; 7.36, etc.). In fact it is probable that healings and exorcisms of Jesus were talked about among the people at a very early stage, even where there was little interest in his exposition of the law or his parables. In the process, at a very early stage they became fused with narratives about other miracle-workers. The raising of the son of a widow in Nain is related in a way analogous to the raising from the dead by the prophets Elijah and Elisha (1 Kings 17; 2 Kings 4), but it also has a parallel in the miracle-worker Apollonius of Tyana, who on one occasion encountered a funeral cortege bearing to the grave a maiden who had died shortly before her marriage. He took hold of the girl's hand and raised her to life (Philostratus, *Vita Apollonii* IV, 45). Josephus offers himself as a witness to an exorcism by one Eleazar in the presence of Vespasian and his officers:

> The healing took place in the following way. He held under the nose of the man possessed a ring containing one of the roots indicated by Solomon, made the sick man sniff it and thus drew out the evil spirit through his nose. The man possessed immediately collapsed, and Eleazar then abjured the spirit never again to return to the man, pronouncing the name of Solomon and the sayings which he composed. (*Ant.* 8, 46–48)

Josephus wrote this down around twenty years after the event and cites witnesses, some of whom were probably still alive. Such stories circulated in many places. Some of their typical features must also have found their way into the narratives about Jesus; indeed whole miracle stories were transferred to him. Here we again detect differences between him and these and other miracle stories. Jesus does not heal on the basis of secret magical traditions, which in the story quoted above are derived from King Solomon. He does not use roots or magical sayings. If a general popular miracle tradition found its way into the tradition about him, we could understand why some of the features typical of him are absent from the miracle stories: for example the notion of following him, the endorsement 'Amen', or the addressing of God as 'Father'.

However, it is characteristic that he attributes to other men and women the power of healing when he says, 'Your faith has saved you' (Mark 5.34).

After Jesus' death, the Jesus tradition was probably handed down in three social contexts: as the tradition of disciples, the community and the people. We should not imagine these as separate circles. What was handed down among the people was also related among followers of Jesus. What was handed down in the settled local communities was also known to itinerant charismatics (i.e. the 'disciples' in the narrower sense). But the core of Jesus' teaching with its radical content was handed down above all by primitive Christian itinerant charismatics in pointed and impressive logia. The local community in Jerusalem probably told of his fate at a very early stage, in the passion story. Tales were told of his miracles throughout the people. The traditions from these various circles was set down in writing in three stages. The tradition of the itinerant charismatics was fixed in the logia source in the first generation. This has a Jewish-Christian stamp throughout. But the tradition of the community and the people was only set down in writing a generation later in the Gentile-Christian Gospel of Mark, around AD 70, and initially combined with some traditions from the itinerant charismatics. Only in the subsequent period (say from 80 to 110) were the two streams of tradition combined in the Gospels of Matthew and Luke: Matthew created a synthesis on the basis of a Jewish Christianity which was open to Gentiles, and Luke on the basis of a Gentile Christianity which was open to Judaism. But before we come to the gospels, we must describe the origin of the second basic form of the New Testament in the first generation, that of the letters.

# CHAPTER 4

# Paul of Tarsus

Soon after the death of Jesus, two currents can be recognized in primitive Christianity. The first signs are tensions in the local community in Jerusalem. According to Acts 6.1ff., there was a conflict there between 'Hebrews' and 'Hellenists', i.e. between Aramaic-speaking and Greek-speaking supporters of Jesus. The rather better educated Hellenists went on the offensive in public. Their leader Stephen was stoned for criticizing the temple. Some of his followers fled into the Hellenized regions of Palestine (including Samaria), and others to Antioch, spreading the Christian faith there. In Antioch they began also to win non-Jews to the Christian faith (Acts 11.20). There they were felt to be an independent group alongside Jews and Gentiles, and for the first time were called 'Christians' (Acts 11.26). In Antioch not only Barnabas but also a former persecutor of Christians by the name of Paul rose to become leaders of the community. After his conversion Paul became particularly keen on opening up the community to Gentiles – perhaps because he had once fought against the Christians, regarding them as 'law-breakers' because of their tendencies towards liberalization. Why did this move-ment towards openness within Judaism become such a problem – first for Paul and then also for other Jews?

The problem was that they put in question the visible signs of Jewish identity: circumcision and the regulations about food. These two ritual signs had become established in the post-exilic period (together with the sanctification of the sabbath) as the decisive identity markers. A dispute over them developed between Jerusalem and Antioch. Around 46/48, in Jerusalem, Barnabas and Paul as delegates from Antioch argued in negotiations with James, Peter and John that circumcision should not be obligatory for non-Jewish members of the community. Paul won this point at the 'Apostolic Council' in Jerusalem (Gal. 2.1–10). It was left open how the second social identity marker of Jews, the regulations about food, was to be dealt with. So shortly afterwards, a conflict broke out all the more vigorously on a return visit of Peter to Antioch (Gal. 2.11–14). Initially Peter ate with Gentile Christians without insisting that the regulations about food should be observed. But when people came from James in Jerusalem, he and Barnabas withdrew from these meals. Probably the delegates from Jerusalem would have been able to point out that Jewish Christians would be put in a difficult situation if Gentile Christians demonstratively also gave up the second Jewish identity marker. Jewish Christians who shared meals with them could then even come under suspicion of apostasy. This time Paul did not win the day, and parted company with Antioch.

But what did the relativizing of the two Jewish identity markers practised by Paul mean for the history of primitive Christianity? These were not petty ritual questions. From that time on Christians were facing the need to develop an independent religion. They could not give new non-Jewish members what was part of any religion in antiquity, namely temple and sacrifice. Because the newly-won Gentile Christians were to worship only the one and only God of the Jews, they were no longer allowed to take part in their pagan temple cults. But they were also forbidden to go to the Jewish temple, because that was bound up with circumcision. Non-Jews were excluded from worshipping in the Jerusalem temple under threat of the death penalty. So Christians had to create a substitute for their Gentile-Christian members: at that time the notion that Christ had been the real once-and-for-all victim became the substitute for the repeated sacrifice in the temple. Baptism then replaced circumcision as the initiation rite.

At the same time these ritual questions had a political dimension. After the Caligula crisis and the indignation that it provoked among the Jews, in AD 41 Claudius had come to power and calmed things down by a policy of the religious status quo. The traditions of Judaism were again to be respected, but they were not to be put in question by Jews either. Claudius sent edicts to this effect to Alexandria, and in Rome too commanded the Jews strictly to adhere to their ancestral traditions; otherwise he would expel them (DioCass. 60, 6, 6). At this very time the Christians began to be active in the Diaspora communities and did precisely what Claudius had forbidden: they deviated from the ancestral traditions and put Jewish identity markers in question. The consensus arrived at in the Apostolic Council around 46/48 furthered their 'liberal' movement. So it is no coincidence that shortly after the Apostolic Council the Christian faith provoked unrest in Rome. Suetonius writes of it: 'Those Jews who, urged on by Chrestus, constantly caused unrest, he (i.e. Claudius) expelled from Rome' (Suetonius, *Claudius* 25, 4). Probably the ring-leaders in these disturbances were expelled. The fugitives rapidly spread news of the unrest among the Jewish communities. Suddenly the Christians were everywhere, troublemakers who opposed Claudius's religious policy (cf. Acts 17.7), especially by taking the line of radical openness to the Gentiles advocated by Paul. Understandably, the situation at the time provided reinforcement for the opponents of Paul who said that it would be better for Christians to remain within Judaism and who required Gentile members, too, to adopt the central marks of Jewish identity, circumcision and the regulations about food. These so-called 'Judaizers' wanted to reverse what Paul had achieved. In this situation Paul developed the letter as the second basic literary form of primitive Christianity; he used it as an instrument for influencing his communities, in order to defend himself against Judaizing opponents. So sometimes Paul has been called the second founder of Christianity. But that is to overestimate him. For he was not the only one to work towards openness for the Gentiles. However, he did lay the intellectual foundations for the development of primitive Christianity into an independent religion alongside Judaism and the preservation of its independence in the 'Judaistic crisis' in the 50s. Who was this Paul, who gave his message of Jesus the form of letters even before the message of Jesus had taken shape in the gospels?

Paul was a Diaspora Jew from Tarsus in Cilicia, who had studied the Torah in Jerusalem and in the process had developed into a Jewish fundamentalist. He writes of his pre-Christian period that his fanatical piety was by no means typical of Judaism: 'And I advanced in Judaism beyond many of my own age among my people, so extremely zealous was I for the traditions of my fathers' (Gal. 1.13). His zeal consisted in persecuting the Jesus movement as a minority deviating from Jewish norms, and at the same time using the disciplinary means of the Jewish communities, expulsion and beatings, on them. Over-emphasis on one's own norms and aggression against minorities who deviate from the norm are the characteristics of an authoritarian religious attitude. Probably Paul was offended that the Christians dreamed of opening up the temple (and the Jewish religion) to all Gentiles and interpreting regulations in the Torah like the commandments about the sabbath and food more liberally than others. But it was particularly scandalous for him that these people appealed to a crucified man who according to the Torah must have been accursed: 'Cursed is anyone who hangs on a tree' (Luke 21.23 = Gal. 3.13). So Paul experienced from the start that veneration of the crucified Jesus and obedience to the Torah were incompatible. He saw the Christian movement as a rebellion against the Jewish law which it was his duty to suppress. When he wanted to extend his oppressive measures to the community in Damascus, he was won over to the new faith which he contested by an appearance of Jesus from heaven – perhaps because previously he had already had hidden doubts about his 'unbroken' pride in the law. Such doubts were present in Judaism. In his *Jewish Antiquities* Josephus paints a vivid picture of the scene in which Zimri rebels against the tyranny of the law of Moses because it forbids him to marry a foreign woman (*Ant.* 4, 141–55). His rebellion is forcibly put down by Phineas, the model zealot. The narrative attests that criticism of the Jewish law was a latent possibility in the Judaism of the time. The encounter with the Risen Christ activated this latent critique of the law in Paul. Criticism of the law as an obstacle to opening Judaism up to the Gentiles became a core of his theology, even if he developed this criticism fully only in later controversies with Judaizers. His conversion turned a Jewish fundamentalist into the leading representative of a universalistic movement of openness in Judaism. An authoritarian believer became the representative of a liberal Judaism – who certainly did not want to found a new religion at that time.

From the beginning Paul was not content to be an ordinary member of the new community. Rather, immediately after his conversion he became a missionary in Arabia, where he worked for around three years (*c.* AD 32–35). His activity there was ended by the war between the Arab Nabataeans and the Galileans. Before this war he retreated to Damascus, pursued by an official of the Nabataean king Aretas, whom he avoided only by being let down the city wall in a basket (2 Cor. 11.32–33) and fleeing to Jerusalem. He arrived there as a political refugee and is hardly likely to have been given an enthusiastic welcome by the Christians whom he had recently been persecuting. At any rate he could speak only with Peter and James the brother of the Lord (Gal. 1.18–19); however, he seems to have convinced these two about himself – the basis of later compromises which he negotiated with them.

In the following period he engaged in missions in Syria and Cilicia, his homeland (according to Gal. 1.21), and later in Cyprus and in southern Asia Minor (Acts 13 – 14). He could have kept questions about the law out of his mission among the Arab Nabataeans. The Nabataeans were circumcised. They believed in a God who was worshipped without images and were accepted as kinsfolk of the Jews (as sons of Ishmael). But Paul could no longer evade these questions on the mission in Syria. For the Antiochene community had accepted Gentiles even before his arrival. Paul became an energetic advocate of their concern to open up Judaism to all Gentiles. Here, in Syrian primitive Christianity, he was moulded as a Christian. We recognize the traces of his socialization there in traditions which he hands on as essentials in his letters. At their centre stood faith in the cross and resurrection. Thus around AD 53 in the first letter to the Corinthians he cites one of these traditions, which shows that historically the appearances of the risen Christ are amazingly well attested. Paul explicitly emphasizes that he has received this tradition, and that it is shared by all the apostles. He mentions by name several witnesses about whom he spoke with Peter and James around two or three years after the appearances. There is no doubt about the subjective authenticity of these reports:

> Now I would remind you, brothers and sisters, of the gospel that I preached to you . . . For I delivered to you as of first importance what I also received, that Christ died for our sins in accordance with the scriptures, that he was buried, that he was raised on the third day in accordance with the scriptures, and that he appeared to Cephas (= Peter), then to the twelve. Then he appeared to more than five hundred brethren at one time, most of whom are still alive, though some have fallen asleep. Then he appeared to James, then to all the apostles. (1 Cor. 15.1, 3–7)

This tradition will have been communicated to him by Syrian Christians after his conversion. From them he learned the language with which he confessed his new faith in simple sentences. In Rom. 10.9–10 he quotes such a confession of faith as a 'word of faith': 'If you confess with your mouth "Jesus is the Lord" and believe in your heart that God has raised him from the dead, you will be saved.' For Paul the decisive thing came to be faith in what God alone can do: call life into being out of nothing. This faith was accessible to all. One does not need to perform specific actions as a Jew to be embraced by him. One has only to acknowledge that God has acted: 'For the scripture says, "No one who believes in him will be put to shame." For there is no distinction between Jew and Greek; the same Lord is Lord of all' (Rom. 10.11ff.).

As we can recognize from such pre-Pauline formulae and confessions in his letters, a Christ piety had developed in the region of Syria even before Paul which differed clearly from the Jesus tradition in Palestine. The basis for this veneration of Christ was not what Jesus had said and done but what God had done with him. Jesus was 'Lord' because God had raised him from the dead. Earthly life became the intermediate stage of a being who had come from heaven and had returned to heaven (Phil. 2.6–11). Paul developed this belief in Christ further. He was not very interested in the words and actions of the earthly Jesus. He quotes only a few sayings of Jesus. Why this striking silence about the earthly Jesus?

First of all a personal reason should be mentioned. Paul had not known the earthly Jesus. Other apostles derived their authority from handing down Jesus' words as his disciples. Paul, who wanted the same status as them, could not compete with them here. He disparaged their knowledge of the earthly Jesus as knowledge by 'human standards' (2 Cor. 5.16). But like the other apostles, Paul had experienced an appearance of the Risen Christ. Here he was on the same footing. No wonder that he puts faith in the Risen Christ at the centre.

In addition there was a reason deriving from social history: the sayings of the earthly Jesus had a radical character that was hardly in place in his communities. Jesus summoned his followers to leave everything; Paul admonished them to remain in the social role in which they had been called (1 Cor. 7.27–28). Jesus promised toll collectors and prostitutes that they would enter the kingdom of God before the pious (Matt. 21.32); Paul excluded prostitutes from the kingdom of God (1 Cor. 6.9). Jesus commanded his disciples to dispense with earning a living and having possessions (Matt. 10.9; 6.25ff.); Paul is proud of earning his own living – and recommends that his communities should also do the same (1 Thess. 2.9; 4.11). Paul orientates his ethical instructions on the needs of the local communities; by contrast the ethic of Jesus is an itinerant radicalism.

However, the decisive reason why Paul is so little interested in the historical Jesus must have been a theological one, namely the basic problem of the new faith with monotheism. On the basis of the Easter appearances Jesus had been experienced as a divine being. That could be claimed within the Judaism of the time only if it was possible to exclude any suspicion that he had claimed this position for himself, so

that he owed it exclusively to God's action. That was the case
in Paul's belief in Christ. A man who has been crucified and
is dead cannot make any claims. Any notion of a self-apotheosis
was ruled out. God alone had exalted him above all names. If
the logia source had ensured by the temptation story that any
suspicion of a self-apotheosis on the part of Jesus had been
excluded, Paul achieved the same purpose by concentrating
on the cross and resurrection. By contrast, stories about a
Jesus who performed miracles or a teacher who spoke with
divine authority could be wrongly understood to indicate that
activity on the part of Jesus was the reason for his worship as a
deity.

Paul developed this theology independently, but with it he
was embedded in early Syrian primitive Christianity. Only as
a result of this could he gain so much influence in Antioch
that along with Barnabas as an authorized delegate of this
community he succeeded in opening up Christianity to the
Gentiles in Jerusalem. In return he promised to make a
collection for the Jerusalem community, to support their poor.
However, at a later date in Antioch he could not win freedom
from all regulations about food. His success in Jerusalem had
motivated him to envisage a worldwide mission. His failure in
Antioch compelled him to carry this out independently. He
began a mission in Europe independent of Antioch.

On this mission, from the start he had probably had Rome
in view as a destination, but even when he was already in
Corinth he was prevented from travelling on there by the
expulsion of Christians from Rome. Indeed the Christians
who had been expelled from Rome were more his supporters
than the conservative Jerusalem Christians. So he remained
in Asia Minor and the Aegean longer than he had planned –
which was why this area became a centre of early Christianity:
in the second generation the first centres, Jerusalem and
Antioch, lost significance to Asia Minor and Rome.

There is controversy over the chronology of Paul's activity
and his letters. There are only a few fixed points for an
absolute chronology. According to Suetonius (in combination
with a note in Orosius) the expulsion of Christians from Rome
took place in the year AD 49. Soon afterwards, in Corinth Paul

met a couple who had been expelled at that time, Aquila and Priscilla (Acts 18.2). They probably shared his open attitude to Gentiles – and in so doing advocated that 'dissolution' of Jewish traditions which was the basis of their expulsion from Rome. He still had a close relationship with them later (Rom. 16.3–4). Supposing that the Apostolic Council took place *c.* 46/48, it must have developed a great missionary dynamic very soon, given that not long afterwards Christianity was present in Macedonia and Greece and was causing unrest in Rome. At all events, *c.* 51/52 Paul was in Corinth. His encounter with the proconsul Gallio falls during his first stay in Corinth (Acts 18.12); it can be dated to spring 52. We can establish Gallio's period in office from the Gallio inscription in the temple of Apollo in Delphi.

There is more dispute over the relative chronology, i.e. the sequence of the letters of Paul and the events of his life. Starting from the fixed dates of the absolute chronology it is possible to argue for the following course of events, but there is no consensus on it:

46–48   As a delegate of the community of Antioch at the Apostolic Council, Paul establishes that Gentile Christians need not be circumcised. In return he promises to make a collection for Jerusalem.

49      On a return visit by Peter to Antioch he cannot carry through the abolition of the regulations over food. So he separates from Antioch and begins an independent mission in Asia Minor and Greece. At the same time Christianity penetrates as far as Rome and there causes unrest in the Jewish community which leads to the expulsion of the 'ringleaders' through the so-called 'edict of Claudius'.

49–50   Paul carries on a mission in Galatia. In Europe his base is the community in Philippi. From there he founds the community in Thessaloniki, where the Christians get into difficulty as troublemakers who are appearing all over the world (including Rome). Paul has to flee.

50–52   Paul arrives in Corinth and there founds a community (Acts 18). He meets the couple Aquila and
Priscilla, who have been expelled from Rome. He
writes 1 Thessalonians from there in 50/51. There
is also unrest in Corinth. However, in spring 52
the Roman proconsul Gallio refuses to start proceedings against Paul.

52–55   Paul transfers the centre of his activity to Ephesus
(Acts 19). From there he makes a journey to
Corinth, the 'interim visit' which turns out badly,
and a journey to Jerusalem and Antioch (Acts
18.22ff.). He writes most of his letters in Ephesus.
There is a serious external and internal crisis
between 1 Corinthians and 2 Corinthians: Paul is
arrested and expects the death penalty, but is
acquitted. At the same time there is a deep conflict in relations with the Corinthian community.
The letters to Philippians and Philemon are composed during his imprisonment. Only the letter to
the Galatians, which also falls into the period in
Ephesus, is difficult to date. It could be either the
second oldest letter after 1 Thessalonians or the
penultimate letter before Romans; thus it could
have been written at the beginning of Paul's stay
in Ephesus or towards the end.

55/56   After his reconciliation with the Corinthians Paul
revisits the community in Corinth. Meanwhile the
emperor Claudius has died (AD 54); the way to
Rome is open. From Rome Paul also wants to
launch a mission to Spain. To prepare for this
visit to Rome and the mission to Spain, in Corinth
Paul writes his letter to the Roman community. In
it, thinking of his imminent journey to Jerusalem
to deliver the collection, he expresses fear for his
life.

56      Paul travels with a delegation from Corinth to
Jerusalem to deliver the collection. The journey
proves to be a disaster.

56–58  Paul is arrested as a notorious lawbreaker; he is imprisoned in Caesarea by the Romans for about two years and then sent to the emperor in Rome.

56–59  He can still be active on behalf of the Christian community even as a prisoner. Some scholars date Philippians and Philemon to this imprisonment in Rome. It is certain that he suffers a martyr's death in Rome, as we know from 1 Clem. 5.4–5.

# CHAPTER 5

# The Beginnings of the Letter Literature in the First Generation: The Letters of Paul

The primitive Christian letter literature was provoked by a crisis. Only after almost two decades of missionary activity from which no letters have been preserved did Paul discover the letter as an instrument for mission and directing the community. He was already familiar with the letter form, since his extant letters (apart from the letter to Philemon) are expanded private letters which presuppose and vary the form of their language. We can observe in Paul a development from the occasional writing governed by the situation (1 Thessalonians) to the beginnings of an early Christian form of publication (Romans).

## 1 Thessalonians – a letter arising out of the situation

Paul founded the community in Thessaloniki in the environs of the Jewish community (Acts 17.1–15). Many godfearers (i.e. non-Jewish sympathizers with Judaism) also joined it. With them the Jewish community lost important points of reference in their pagan environment. Moreover they felt that the Christians were a political danger which could discredit them publicly. That emerges from the charge lodged by Gentile fellow-citizens with the magistrate on their urging:

- 'These people who have set the whole world in an uproar are now also here' (Acts 17.6). So Christians have already been prominent in other places.

- 'They have all offended against the laws of the emperor.' But they are accused only of one specific crime: 'They claim that there is another king, namely Jesus' (17.7).

- The charge of financial irregularities must also have played a role, since the Christians had to post bail (17.9).

Probably news of the unrest in Rome in AD 49 had reached Thessaloniki. This report could in fact have given the impression that Christians were causing disturbances 'all over the world' (i.e. also in Rome). To avoid disturbances in their city the Jewish community had Paul accused (by loyal god-fearers?). So in 1 Thess. 2.14–16 he reacts with sharp polemic against 'the Jews' who are hindering his mission to the Gentiles, although he sees their Gentile fellow-citizens as the real opponents of the young community (2.14). The charge criticizes the opposition to the religious policy of Claudius and his 'edicts' (in the plural), and charges Christians with proclaiming Jesus as king. It presupposes that Jesus is a royal pretender who is still alive. It does not indicate that this is worship of someone who has risen from the dead. The same misunderstanding can also be glimpsed in Suetonius' note about the expulsion of the Christians from Rome. But this particular misunderstanding is 'understandable': in 1 Thess. 4.15–16 the 'arrival' of the Lord is in fact depicted as being like the transporting of a ruler from heaven to earth. Since Paul is accused of financial fraud (because of the collection that he is making?), he asserts his integrity and says that he has earned his living with the work of his own hands (2.9) – just as the Thessalonians, too, are not to cheat anyone (4.6) but are to 'work with their own hands' (4.11–12). The admonitions to take work seriously are so clear in 1 Thessalonians that we are to assume that corresponding accusations lie in the background.

Why does Paul write his letter? After the accusation he had had to leave the community in a hurry (Acts 17.10) and had travelled to Corinth. Other Christians had to carry the can in the court hearing that he had provoked. We can see Paul's guilt feelings in the letter. He describes himself as 'orphaned' (2.17), as if it was not he who had abandoned the community but the community which had abandoned him – although he wants to be its 'mother' (2.7). The vigorous outburst against 'the Jews' (2.14–16) is intended to conjure up a common opponent to bring him and the community together. He assures them that he is being as much persecuted by the Jews as they are being persecuted by their Gentile fellow-citizens. He has a real longing to see the community (2.17) and to assure himself that his relationship with them is not damaged. Because he cannot come in person, he sends Timothy to Thessaloniki with a letter.

In this letter Paul has (for the first time?) expanded the form of the private letter so that it becomes a letter to the community. The so-called *prooemium* (= preface) stylistically affirms his good relationship with those whom he is addressing. Paul expands this part, which is orientated on his relationship with the Thessalonians. He duplicates his typical motifs: twice he assures the Thessalonians that he is praying for them (1.2; 3.12–13), twice he praises their exemplary character (1.6ff.; 3.13ff.), and twice he makes his relationship to them the theme.

The second part of the letter contains admonitions in which he defines Christian identity by setting it apart from the world around. Paul shows that being a Christian consists in faith, love and hope (1.3; 5.8; 3.6–13). He had already defined *faith* in the 'living God' in the introduction to the letter as turning away from the gods of the surrounding world and as the expectation of God's 'son', who has been raised from the dead (1.8–10). In the closing part of the letter he emphasizes the 'sanctification' of the Christians as what marks them out from those around them. This sanctification is manifested negatively in overcoming the 'passionate desires' of the

Gentiles (4.3ff.) and positively in '*love of the brethren*' (Greek *philadelphia*, 4.9), a word which appears here for the first time in a metaphorical sense. In 1 Thessalonians 'brotherliness' is attested for the first time as the designation of an ethic of solidarity. Finally, Christians do not react to death in a depressed way, 'like the others, who have no hope' (4.13). Those who had just been converted had hoped that they would experience the advent of the Lord in their lifetimes. Meanwhile, however, some of them had died (4.13). We need not postulate any martyrs here. Probably some seriously ill people had also joined the new Christian movement, who fervently hoped that Christ would very soon overcome the world which had fallen victim to death. But Paul had fled before he could communicate to the community his belief in the resurrection of the dead. Now he comforts those who have been left behind. The dead will not be at a disadvantage at the coming of the Lord. He still expresses an ardent expectation of an imminent end. But he puts at the centre a notion which is independent of this and which persists in all his letters: the dead and the living will be 'with Christ' (4.17; 5.10). What happened to Christ happens to them in death. This fellowship with Christ is the decisive content of his hope.

The situation to which we owe the first (extant) community letter was an extraordinary one. The letter replaced oral communication after a forced parting. Paul has some inkling of the potential of the letter for guiding the community. Therefore he urges those whom he is addressing to 'read out this letter to all the brethren' (5.27). He does not want it to be a private letter to leaders or to a minority who can read. His admonition would be superfluous if the genre of the community letter had already been established. It is still in the making.

## The anti-Judaizing letters: Galatians and Philippians

### (a) Galatians

Paul discovered the power of the letter at the latest when he had to contest a counter-mission. This mission was reacting

to the political difficulties of the Jewish community caused
by the Christians, as these became evident in the edict of
Claudius. According to the edict, Jewish groups were forbidden to change Jewish traditions. Therefore the anti-Pauline
counter-mission aimed at reintegrating the Christian communities into Judaism. It encountered them for the first
time in Galatia. Since the Apostolic Council there had been
a consensus that Gentile Christians did not have to adopt
circumcision, but there was no obligation for Gentiles to
accept circumcision anyway. Anyone could do that voluntarily.
Politically it would have been an advantage. The religious
policy under Claudius, which sought to prevent any devia-
tion by the Jews from the customs of their ancestors, would
have been satisfied, and tensions with the Jewish community
would have been reduced. In Galatians Paul rightly implies
that his opponents wanted to use circumcision merely in order
to avoid conflict, so that they 'are not persecuted' (5.12). And
he suggests that these opponents are fundamentally indifferent about the observance of all the regulations of the
law (5.3). In fact the primary issue was simply the two ritual
identity markers of Judaism.

Exegetes often see Paul's opponents merely as sworn
enemies of openness to the Gentiles. But Paul's polemic does
not lead us to expect that he is treating their motives fairly.
Probably they were more harmless than Paul portrays them
as being. If they had been able to gain influence in his communities, this would not have been by denouncing their
founder, but by appealing to him: Paul had made a beginning
with his preaching and they wanted to complete his work
through circumcision. There was a model for such a two-stage
mission in Judaism: the first move from being a Gentile to
the Jewish faith often merely meant individuals visiting
synagogue services as 'godfearers' without being circumcised.
They (or the next generation) went over to Judaism fully only
by circumcision. Possibly some Jewish Christians at the
Apostolic Council already had this model in view when they
accepted the Antiochene mission which did not involve
circumcision. They recognized Paul's work as a preliminary
stage towards full entry into the community. But Paul is certain

that his mission was fully recognized. It was not just a preliminary stage, to be completed by circumcision. In every
respect it was on an equal footing with the mission to Israel.
Faced with the subtle twisting of his message and the agreements at the Apostolic Council he appeals in perplexity to
the Galatians: 'Are you so foolish? Having begun with the
Spirit, are you now ending with the flesh (i.e. with circumcision)?' (3.3). The Galatians must have sensed that the new
missionaries were not working along the same lines as Paul.
They sent messengers to Paul (to Ephesus?). And Paul made
it clear that the new missionaries were not completing his
work but destroying it. It was not the opponents who were
driving a wedge between Paul and the community, but Paul
who was driving a wedge between the community and his
opponents.

Because since the Apostolic Council circumcision had not
been obligatory, the opponents had to build on voluntary
action – and therefore strengthen their 'ideological' justification even further. They had to revalue the Jewish law.
Adopting it (through circumcision) was to be the consummation of faith. In a counter-move Paul criticizes the law in a
form which is intolerable for Jews. The law came into the
world only 430 years after the promise to Abraham, and
applies only until the coming of the messiah (3.6–18). It
is not directly of divine origin, but was only communicated
by angels; it has no power to create life, but was added to
the promise only 'for the sake of sins' (3.19) – as a protection from sins, to disclose sins or even to provoke them.
Dependence on it is compared with slavery (4.1ff.; 4.21ff.)
and with pagan dependence on the elements of the world
(4.3). Paul wants to show that if the Galatians adopted the
law they would not be completing their faith but lapsing
into their paganism (4.8ff.). It is not progress but a retro-
grade step.

But at the same time Paul skilfully takes up the Galatians'
longing to complete their faith. The law is summed up in the
commandment to love (Lev. 19.18 = Gal. 5.14). It must be
observed. But to observe it one needs only the power of the
Spirit, the first-fruit of which is love (5.22). What Christians

do spontaneously, driven by the Spirit, does not contradict the law, and is at the same time its real fulfilment. For the Spirit roots the social intention of the law in the hearts of Christians, so that they fulfil the commandments spontaneously. They no longer need the law as a 'tutor' (a chaperone to take young children to school) which makes them fulfil it from outside (3.24). Through love the Galatians may fulfil their faith through the 'law of Christ' (= 'the law of the messiah') (Gal. 6.2).

Thus a dispute over ritual questions leads in Galatians to a fundamental ambivalence towards the law. On the one hand a negative view has to be taken of it. It is opposed to the promise. Fulfilling the law cannot bring salvation. The summary of Paul's doctrine of justification says this in the statement that 'man is not justified by works of the law but through faith in Jesus Christ' (2.16). On the other hand, the law is to be judged positively. It is fulfilled in the commandment to love (5.13ff.). Both statements stand side by side in juxtaposition. In the relationship to God the law has been superseded, but in relations with fellow men and women it is indispensable.

In Galatians we can observe how the community letter explodes the form of the private letter. Basically it is a speech in Paul's defence. After an introduction (*exordium*) (1.6–11) Paul begins with a *narratio*, which explains the conflict historically with remarks about Paul's life and the history of primitive Christianity (1.12 – 2.14). This issues in a *propositio*: here Paul pointedly sums up the doctrine of justification as his thesis (2.15–21). The proof or *probatio* follows in two parallel trains of thought on Christians as children of Abraham: the first argument (3.1 – 4.7) focuses on the fact that with the fulfilment of the promise to Abraham all differences between 'Jew and Greek, slave and free, man and woman' are overcome in Christ (Gal. 3.28). For Christ alone is the descendant of Abraham. The promise applies to him. Anyone who is 'in him' has a share in its fulfilment. Here the motivation for the criticism of the law is that it separates people. The second argument (4.8–31) shows that children of Abraham are split into hostile groups: the children of the freewoman, Sarah, and the children of the slave girl, Hagar. For Jews the identification of Jews with the children of Hagar is unacceptable (this term is usually applied to the Arabs), as is the identification of Christians with the children of Sarah (this is usually applied to the Jews). However, for Paul Christianity is Judaism rightly understood. Therefore for him unbelieving Jews often take the role of Gentiles, and Gentile Christians the role of Jews. Thus according to the first argument, being a child of Abraham leads to the overcoming of social differences and at the same time according to the second argument to new enmities! In Galatians the contradiction between these conclusions from being a child of Abraham remains unresolved. The *probatio* is followed by an admonition (*exhortatio*), which does not belong to the legal speech (5.1 – 6.10). Here the letter form is established. Paul writes the *conclusio* in his own hand.

The introduction makes it clear that Paul's 'apologia', formulated in virtuoso style, bursts open the traditional letter form. The *prooemium,* which is meant to emphasize the close links between the writer and those whom he is addressing, becomes a caricature. In its place we read two curses: 'If anyone preaches to you another gospel than we have preached, let him be accursed' (1.8), and 'If anyone preaches to you another gospel than that which you received, let him be accursed' (1.9). Towards the end of the letter Paul uses the duplication technique from 1 Thessalonians: twice he introduces an admonition with the motif of freedom: 'For freedom Christ has set us free; stand fast, therefore, and do not submit again to a yoke of slavery' (5.1). And he repeats: 'You were called to freedom, brethren; only do not use your freedom as an opportunity for the flesh, but through love be servants of one another' (5.13). At the end he imitates legal documents of his time, which were signed in a person's own hand, thus gaining legal validity. The letter is enriched by elements from other genres and thus becomes a genuinely primitive Christian literary genre. Clichés from rhetoric show that Paul must have had a modest education.

## (b) Philippians

Philippians also belongs among the anti-Judaizing letters – at least in its middle part (Phil. 3). There is argument over a number of questions relating to it. Where was it written? In Ephesus or in Rome? Is it a single letter or a letter composed of fragments? The only thing that we can be sure of is that Paul wrote the letter in prison. But where was he? Paul was arrested three times: in Ephesus, Caesarea and Rome. There was a lively exchange between him and those to whom he wrote: Epaphroditus came with a gift, but fell ill, and news about this disturbed the Philippians (2.26). When he recovered Paul send him back with a letter of thanks (4.10–20). He said that he himself would come soon (2.24). The lively exchange fits the distance between Philippi and Ephesus, but not that between Rome and Caesarea. Above all the visit which Paul announces tells against Rome. For from Rome Paul wanted to go to Spain. Since a 'praetorium' also does not necessarily indicate Rome (cf. Mark 15.16) and people 'from the emperor's house' (4.22) were not to be found only there, Philippians is more likely to have been written in Ephesus than in Rome.

Philippians is a letter of friendship. Paul has excellent relations with the community in Philippi. After he had lost Antioch as his home community, it had become the basis of his mission in Europe (4.15), from which he accepted material support (contrary to his principle of economic independence). Paul has developed this letter of friendship into a community letter. He has two topics in it: his trial before a Roman governor and the appearance of Judaizing missionaries in the community in Philippi. He copes with both by working out his conformity with Christ and in this way making himself a model for the community.

Paul may be in prison. But even if he had to die, he knows that in death he will be directly with Christ (1.20–26). He had still seen things differently in 1 Thessalonians. There the dead had to wait for the Lord's parousia in order to rise. Confrontation with the personal danger of death led him to change his hope about the world to come: the future hope becomes the certainty of a new life which begins immediately after death. What is decisive for Paul is that after his possible execution he will be with Christ. But even now he is associated with Christ as a prisoner. In his prison cell he strikes up the Philippians hymn, which sings of how Christ as a divine being humbled himself to death on a cross (and thus is near to the imprisoned Paul, threatened with execution), in order to be exalted by God above all other powers – even above the powers in whose hands Paul now is. Even if the Romans had him executed, Paul knows that one day they will have to join with all other peoples and powers in bowing the knee to his Lord (2.10). The Philippians hymn is a defiant song against the humiliation of prison. At the same time Paul uses it to guide the community: if, like Christ, all Christians renounce their status, they will be able to cope with rivalry and conflicts with one another (2.1ff.).

In the third chapter Paul combats the danger from Judaizing opponents in a tone which has suddenly changed. Consequently, time and again it has been conjectured that this chapter is the fragment of another letter which has been worked into a friendly letter here. Judaizing opponents have penetrated to Europe. We do not hear that they require the Philippians to be circumcised and to observe the regulations about food. Perhaps on this point they were more cautious than those in Galatia. But they showed such great pride in these Jewish marks of identity that Paul accuses them of having their belly as their god (thus caricaturing their overestimation of the food laws) and their 'shame' as their boasting (here he is disparaging their pride in the circumcision of their sexual organs, which in 3.2 he mocks as castration) (3.19). Moreover these opponents, too, want to 'complete' Christianity, which is why Paul emphasizes that he is still on the way to his goal (3.12). Here, too, Paul copes with the problem through conformity with Christ: with Christ Paul has left his former Jewish days behind him (3.7–11). Through conformity with Christ he has been changed and will be changed in the future (3.20–21). The community is to imitate him here (3.17). Just as he has radically rejected his former days with all their privileges, so too the community is to reject the Judaizing opponents with all their 'privileges'. Paul shows that the privileges of his Jewish days, Jewish descent, fulfilment of the law and zeal, have faded, indeed have become worthless, in the face of the knowledge of Jesus Christ.

Again Paul succeeds in discussing fundamental problems of Christian faith and life in a letter dictated by the situation – and also by inserting a different genre from that of Philippians – so that it become possible to understand why this letter has had an influence independently of its original context.

### (c) Philemon

Although not an anti-Judaizing letter, this was also written in Ephesus. It comes closest to a private letter, but is not one. After a dispute (or a misfortune) Philemon's slave Onesimus had sought Paul out in prison – not to escape slavery by flight but to ask him to mediate as a friend of his master. That was not unusual. Paul converts him to the Christian faith and sends him back with a diplomatic letter. Part of the diplomacy lies in the fact that Paul addresses this letter to the household community of Philemon and thus expresses the expectation that Philemon will not treat the problem as a private matter but resolve it in the context of the community. For the same reason he announces that he will pay a visit. So Philemon will have to justify himself before him and the community! What Paul expects of Philemon is that he will accept Onesimus 'no longer as a slave but as far more: as a beloved brother . . . as a man and also before the Lord' (Philemon 16). So Paul is thinking not only of a new religious relationship 'in the Lord' but of a new relationship in everyday reality ('in the flesh'). Now at that time there was a model solution for such conflicts: the slave was sold to a new master. Why should not Paul have bought Onesimus' freedom if he had wanted to help him? In fact Paul wants to have Onesimus transferred so that Onesimus can serve him as a fellow-worker on the mission – just as other communities put such fellow-workers at his disposal – but he will not (or cannot) pay anything for him. He simply wants to make good the harm done to Onesimus: 'I, Paul, write this with my own hand; I will repay it – to say nothing of your owing me even your own self' (Philemon 19). In other words, it would be quite inappropriate for Paul to have to pay anything – either for limited damage or for the person of Onesimus. For Philemon is himself in debt to the apostle. He can repay this debt by transferring Onesimus to Paul: 'Yes, brother, I want some benefit from you in the Lord. Refresh my heart in Christ' (Philemon 20). Here slavery is not being put in question as an institution: Paul is dealing only with an individual case. But his expectation that slaves should be treated as brothers is a remarkable step beyond the average mentality of a 'slave-owner society'. And it is certainly not meant to hold only for this individual instance. Even a brotherly relationship with freemen would have been unusual. They too remained dependents who continued to have a duty to perform services for their master. Therefore to treat a slave as a brother in a sense means more than to free him. Since the household slaves in cities were in any case freed at around the age of thirty if they had good masters, this is not Paul's topic. Moreover Seneca argued similarly for the humane treatment of slaves (*Ep.mor.* 47). But he makes this dependent on the personal morality of shareowners and the moral quality of the slave. He does not intervene in slavery as an institution. By contrast, the letter to Philemon is evidence of a religious community intervening in the affairs of a private household. The community exerts its social force through its apostle: 'Though I am bold enough in Christ to command you to do what is required, yet for love's sake I prefer to appeal to you – I, Paul, an old man, and now a prisoner also for Christ Jesus . . .' (Philemon 8 – 9). Probably Paul got his way. We later find an Onesimus in his entourage (Col. 4.9).

### The anti-enthusiastic letters: the letters to the Corinthians

Around the time that Paul was fighting against Judaizers in Galatia and Philippi, he was grappling with enthusiasts in Corinth. His Corinthian correspondence comprises three letters, probably more. He mentions two letters which have not been preserved: a letter which has been understood as a call to Christians to separate themselves from the world and which he has to correct in 1 Corinthians (1 Cor. 5.9), and a letter written in tears after a deep injury which a Corinthian has done to him (2 Cor. 2.4). It is possible that parts of this letter have been preserved in 2 Corinthians: the 'separation letter' in 6.14–17 in which Paul admonishes his readers to 'separate from them . . .' (6.17); and the tearful letter in 10 – 13, in which an insulted Paul abruptly criticizes his opponents and the community, although previously he had become reconciled with the community (5.11 – 6.13; 7.2–4). In fact 2 Corinthians looks like a letter composed of heterogeneous parts. The best hypothesis seems to be that it should be divided into parts. Perhaps people in Corinth had the ambition of setting an equally long second letter alongside 1 Corinthians, composing it of different letters of Paul's.

### (a) Paul and the community in Corinth

Paul had a special relationsip with the community in Corinth. When he fled from Thessaloniki, he went via Athens to Corinth, where he met Aquila and Priscilla, who had been banished from Rome. There he founded a large, pre-dominantly Gentile-Christian, community. We know more about its life than about that of any other community. Acts 18.1–17 tells us about its foundation phase. Where Acts stops, the Corinthian correspondence begins. The historical recon-struction of events differs. The following survey does not claim to represent the only possibility, but does not represent an extreme position.

- The *first beginnings in Corinth* were a meeting between Paul and the Christians Aquila and Priscilla, whose position was close to his; they had been expelled from Rome by the edict of Claudius (Acts 18.1–4). Initially he lived (in their house) by earning his own living as a craftsman (1 Cor. 4.12) and taught in the synagogue.

- There was a *separation from the synagogue* (Acts 18.5–8): Silas and Timothy came from Macedonia. They brought a gift (cf. Phil. 4.15–16), so that Paul could devote himself wholly to the mission. After he had been rejected in the synagogue he moved to the house of Titius Justus, a godfearer, who lived near the synagogue. Paul converted the Jewish synagogue president Crispus along with his house (cf. 1 Cor. 1.14) and won many adherents. The community was predominantly Gentile-Christian. Paul remained in Corinth for eighteen months.

- The *trial before Gallio* comes at the end of Paul's first stay in Corinth (Acts 18.12–17): Paul is accused by Jews of worshipping God 'contrary to the law'. Gallio does not allow the charge. As the spokesman of the Jewish community the president of the synagogue (who has meanwhile replaced Crispus, who has converted to Christianity?) is maltreated in the presence of Gallio. Paul then travels (with Priscilla and Aquila) to Ephesus, and from there to Jerusalem, Antioch and back to Ephesus.

- In *Apollos*, Paul has a rival in his community (Acts 18.27–28; cf. 1 Cor. 1.12). This teacher, originally from Alexandria, came to Corinth from Ephesus and returned there. Paul vainly asked him to make a new journey to Corinth (1 Cor. 16.12ff.). The correspondence between Paul and the Corinthians began at this time.

- A first letter, the *separation letter*, is mentioned in 1 Cor. 5.9ff. It calls for separation from all 'fornication, avarice, etc.', but is understood as an invitation to separate from the world generally. Part of it could be preserved in 2 Cor. 6.14 – 7.1, where Paul calls in an unusually sharp way for Christians to separate from their pagan environment.

- The Corinthians write a *community letter* to Paul asking whether Paul really requires this sharp separation from the world in every respect. Their questions can be recognized in 1 Corinthians in a stereotyped 'on this point it has to be said' (*peri de*). There are enquiries about asceticism (1 Cor. 7.1ff.), about young women not getting married (7.25ff.), about eating meat offered to idols (8.1ff.), about the gifts of the Spirit (12.1ff.), about the collection (16.1ff.) and about Apollos (16.12).

- *1 Corinthians* is Paul's answer to the community letter. Its content can be summed up with the three words faith, love and hope (1 Cor. 13.13). (1) The message of the cross is regarded as the decisive foundation of *faith* (1 Cor. 1 – 4). (2) *Love* and constructive social behaviour ('edification') are guidelines for behaviour (1 Cor. 8 – 14) in questions of sexuality, eating (including the eucharist), and language, which has become a problem because of incomprehensible glossolalia (1 Cor. 5.7, 8 – 11, 12 – 14). (3) At the end Paul discusses Christian *hope* as expectation of the resurrection from the dead (1 Cor. 15). Thus two of Paul's central themes, cross and resurrection, frame 1 Corinthians (cf. 1 – 4; 15).

- New rival *missionaries* dramatically change the situation after 1 Corinthians. They come with letters of commendation (2 Cor. 2.17; 3.1; 5.12). In Corinth Paul is compared with these 'super apostles' and is mocked as a comparatively 'weak' apostle (12.11).

- Paul wants to save his authority by an *interim visit* (cf. 2 Cor. 2.1–2). It is a disaster. A member of the community insults him grievously (2 Cor. 2.5–11; 7.12). Perhaps this insult has been preserved in 2 Cor. 10.10: 'His bodily presence is weak and his speech of no account.' Paul travels back deeply hurt.

- From Ephesus he writes the *tearful letter*, so-called after the letter mentioned in 2 Cor. 2.4, written in 'tears'. This is a desperate attempt even now to overcome the rift. It is perhaps contained in 2 Cor. 10 – 13. And indeed some do side with him (2 Cor. 2.14 – 7.4) (see below).

- *Imprisonment in Ephesus* (cf. 2 Cor. 1.9; Phil. 1) becomes a great crisis for Paul. He certainly expects the death sentence. Surprisingly he is acquitted (2 Cor. 9.1–2).

To bring about a reconciliation with the Corinthians he sends Titus as an intermediary to Corinth and travels back to Macedonia after him. When Titus arrives there with good news, in Macedonia Paul writes

- the *letter of reconciliation* which is contained in 2 Cor. 1.1 – 2.13; 7.5–16 (= 8). In it 2.14 – 7.4 (without 6.14 – 7.1) is an apologia for Paul's apostleship, which is usually regarded as part of the letter of reconciliation after the ending of the conflict. But it is also given another position, either as part of a letter before the interim visit, as a first still relaxed reaction by Paul to rivals, or as part of the tearful letter at the height of the conflict. 2 Cor. 9 is perhaps an independent letter to promote the collection.

In Corinth, the problems which Paul had to deal with were not those in his anti-Judaizing letters. In them he had engaged in controversy with opponents and fought against the law, because he could not acknowledge it in some ritual questions. Over against the law he set the Spirit as the force that shaped Christian life: 'If we live by the Spirit then let us also follow the Spirit' (Gal. 5.25). And he had appealed to a direct bond with Christ: his admonition 'Be so disposed to one another as befits a life in Christ Jesus' (Phil. 2.5) is characteristic. Paul himself argues in these letters like an 'enthusiast', i.e. like someone who trusts that God dwells in people through his Spirit and transforms them into new beings. But in Corinth he had to do with people who shared his enthusiasm. Here he had to correct the consequences of his own message, not with opponents, but with his own followers. For the Corinthians the Spirit was a miraculous heavenly power which expressed itself in speaking with tongues and extraordinary gifts, and which even now made people 'float' in a life beyond everyday life. Ecstatic experiences were regarded as key religious experiences. Here Paul had to damp down the enthusiasm that he himself verged on in Galatians. He wanted to show the Corinthians that an intense experience of the divine presence in the Spirit is not the decisive factor; the decisive thing is how one directs the energy of the Spirit for the well-being of one's fellow men and women. So he has to formulate imperatives.

The need to intervene more in regulating community life arose from two factors, as a result of which the religious 'enthusiasm' in Corinth could have destructive effects. (1) The community was not socially homogeneous, but comprised different strata and cultures. (2) Missionaries coming from outside reinforced the internal tensions. Here the conflicts increased between 1 Corinthians and 2 Corinthians, because after 1 Corinthians new missionaries had arrived.

1. The community was mixed socially: there were a few dominant figures who were better off, and many ordinary people (1 Cor. 1.26). This difference became notable in questions about openly taking part in pagan cultic meals. Ordinary people ate meat above all in a cultic setting, i.e. at festivals and public distributions of meat. The better off bought it in the macellum (in 1 Cor. 10.25), the specialist butcher's shop of the ancient cities, which was frequented predominantly by the rich. Meat which had not been ritually slaughtered could also be bought there. So for ordinary people, eating meat was far more bound up with idolatry than for the rich. Therefore if the rich advocated their liberal position with enthusiastic slogans –'We are free', 'Everything is permissible for us' – fellowship could be destroyed. Paul suggests to them that they should voluntarily abstain from eating meat offered to idols, but allows them to consume it in private if none of those present understands the meal as a cultic action. Class-specific problems also arose at the celebration of the eucharist. In antiquity, at shared feasts the rich were accustomed to give their freemen and clients worse food than they ate themselves. These (and other) bad practices also seem to have found their way into the Christian community. Here Paul emphatically says that those who put the have-nots to shame at the eucharist offend against its meaning. Everyone may eat their fill at home (1 Cor. 11.17–34).

2. Rival missionaries were the second factor which accentuated the crisis. They are already a problem in 1 Corinthians. Unlike Paul they allowed themselves to be supported by the community – referring to Jesus' instructions that missionaries should not provide for themselves. Paul has to defend himself because he works with his hands and accepts no money (1 Cor. 9.1ff.). Among his rivals, Apollos in particular was a talented orator whose wisdom impressed the Corinthians. For Peter's supporters their master was above all 'the foundation of the church'. Paul's supporters could only point out that he had founded the community. Of course the different supporters each praised the features that marked their apostle out: the supporters of Apollos praised his wisdom; the supporters of Peter the fact that he was the foundation of the church (cf. 1 Cor. 3.11); the supporters of Paul necessarily had a high appreciation of baptism as the beginning of the Christian life which associated them with their apostle. But Paul had to point out to them that he had baptized only a very few people (1 Cor. 1.16). He does not think much of the way in which they form parties, even if one party swears by him. He has even offended some of his own supporters. No wonder that the situation has dramatically deteriorated in the second letter. New missionaries with letters of commendation have arrived. Over and above the rivals in 1 Corinthians they introduce a Judaizing emphasis into the debate. For they present themselves as representatives of a spiritual Israel and as true descendants of Abraham (2 Cor. 11.22). Perhaps they advocated a pneumatic exegesis of the law (2 Cor. 3.1ff.). But they no longer strive to reintegrate Christians into Judaism by adopting ritual demands. These are more moderate opponents than those in Galatia and Philippi, Either they have toned down their demands on the way to Corinth or they are representatives of the 'more moderate' wing of the Jewish Christians. But they too want a reintegration of Christians into Judaism, though they are content to adopt a spiritual

self-understanding – and that ran counter to the
Corinthians, who were moved by the Spirit. Perhaps for
all of them Moses was a figure bathed in divine
splendour, and the law was a spiritual entity (cf. 2 Cor.
3.6ff.). At all events, compared with these apostles Paul
does not seem to have been an impressive figure: he
was no great orator (2 Cor. 10.10), no admirable ecstatic
(12.1ff.), no powerful miracle worker (12.11–12.), but
rather a sick man whom God had not healed (12.7ff.).
In short, he was a weak charismatic. But the rival apostles
were full of spirit and charisma in the sense of an
impressively irrational aura. If in 1 Corinthians Paul had
written to mediate between conflicts in the community,
2 Corinthians bears witness to a conflict between him
and the community: he has to defend himself. Therefore
2 Corinthians is his most personal letter.

Now that I have described the situation of the Corinthian
community for the two letters in a summary, I want to look at
each of the letters to the Corinthians independently.

### (b) 1 Corinthians

In response to the conflicts in the community, in 1 Corinthians
Paul develops his understanding of community and in
2 Corinthians his understanding of himself as an apostle. In
2 Corinthians there is only one theme: the apostle's relationship to the community, but in 1 Corinthians he discusses a
wealth of specific questions. Round the discussion of these
points he puts a framework made up of remarks on two central
themes of his preaching, cross and resurrection.

The little sermon at the beginning 'on the meaning of the
cross' is a masterpiece (1 Cor 1.18ff.). Paul develops its
meaning (as in the Philippians hymn) without the notion of
an atoning death. The cross is the basis of salvation because
God has done away with every criterion of power, status and
wisdom through it. He chooses the lowly and those without
rights when he identifies himself with someone who has
been executed as a criminal. Through the cross he creates a

fundamental freedom towards the criteria of the world (i.e. society). So in discussing the topics which follow, Paul time and again aims at freeing Christians from such criteria without losing their capacity to engage in dialogue with the environment. Faith is faith in the cross as a revolutionary action of God, in which he has allied himself with the 'rulers of this world' (1 Cor. 2.6, 8).

At the end of the letter, in a brief discussion he defends hope of the resurrection. It frees people from fear even in the most difficult situations, if like Paul one has to 'fight with wild beasts', which must be meant metaphorically (1 Cor. 15.32). Some people in Corinth denied the resurrection of the body. For them the body was transitory and not the inner nucleus of human beings. Over against this Paul sets another understanding of corporeality: the whole person will be transformed. The earthly body will be transformed into a 'spiritual' body. That reinforces the admonitions in Corinthians to take seriously all that pertains to the body: sexuality, eating, and the tongue, which gets out of control in glossolalia.

These basic statements are surrounded by a series of remarks in which these three human communicative actions become a concern: sexuality (1 Cor. 5.1 – 7.40); eating, including the eucharist (1 Cor. 8 – 11); and language (1 Cor. 14). Paul always has to find a balance between demarcation from the environment and assimilation to it.

In sexual questions Paul contests, for example, the practice of men visiting prostitutes, which was taken for granted (1 Cor. 6.12ff.). At the same time, against ascetic currents he argues for the right of marriage as a Christian life form, even if he regards remaining unmarried as the better way, though it is not for everyone (1 Cor. 7.1ff.). Alongside this a third form of life is being pioneered: the cohabitation of unmarried couples without engaging in sexual intercourse (1 Cor. 7.25ff.). The criterion for action is a high esteem for the body as a temple of the spirit of Christ. The body is not something to be indifferent about. What happens to it affects one's own identity.

In questions relating to food he wants to drive a wedge between the cultic meals in the environment and the Lord's Supper. The two are incompatible (1 Cor. 10.14–22). But at the same time he is looking for ways of making it possible to share meals with Gentiles in private (1 Cor. 10.23ff.). In other words, food as an expression of social communication between people is exempt from any kind of rule, but as the expression of a cultic action it is subject to the religious norms of the community. There is a borderline case when one person regards eating as merely a social act but others understand it as a religious action. In that case it would be better to renounce eating together. The criterion for action is on the one hand love and on the other respect for the conscience, above all that of the other person.

In questions of language Paul wants to integrate glossolalia, which makes Christians suspect of being crazy (1 Cor. 14.23), into community life without suppressing it (1 Cor. 12 – 14). For ethical orientation he offers an image and a criterion: the image is the 'body of Christ', in which all human beings are like members of a body and in which the weakest member (and not the strongest member, as in many variants on this image in antiquity) needs to be taken note of. The criterion is love. For him love is the highest gift of the Spirit. It replaces all longing for ecstatic peak experiences. Often religious gifts and insights are nothing. To inculcate this he writes his famous hymn to love (1 Cor. 13.11ff.):

> If I speak in the tongues of men and of angels,
> but have not love,
> I am a noisy gong or a clanging symbol.
> And if I have prophetic powers
> and understand all mysteries and all knowledge,
> and if I have all faith, so as to remove mountains,
> but have not love,
> I am nothing.
> If I give away all I have, and if I deliver my body to be burned,
> but have not love,
> I gain nothing . . .

### (c) 2 Corinthians

In 2 Corinthians Paul develops his 'self-understanding' as an apostle in response to attacks by rival missionaries. The letter is stamped by a great tension between a sense of authority and a sense of inferiority. On the one hand Paul has an exalted task as representative of a new era, as servant of the spirit and not the letter (3.1 – 4.6). The Spirit renews a person in Christ to become a 'new creature' (5.17). The content of this new covenant is 'reconciliation' not only with Israel but with the whole world. Here Paul reinterprets the cross once again: it means more than atonement for sins; it creates reconciliation. God sends messengers as if to mediate between conflicting parties, to make peace between himself and human beings. Through the apostle he asks people to 'be reconciled with God' (5.20). This reconciliation is the restoration of a personal relationship – and thus more than expiation, with which a destroyed legal order is restored.

Alongside this sense of authority there is a sense of inferiority. Paul says of himself and his great task, 'We have this treasure in earthen vessels' (4.7). The grace of God 'shows its power in weakness' (12.9). Weakness includes Paul's sickness (perhaps a migraine, which would pierce the head like a 'thorn'). They also include his suffering and persecutions (4.7ff.; 11.24ff.). In them Paul knows that he is close to Christ. So, *talking as a fool*, he can boast of his weaknesses: 'He (Christ) may have been crucified in his weakness but he lives by the power of God. We too are weak in him, but together with him before your eyes we will live by God's power' (13.4). Because of this nearness of Christ Paul is certain that he will win over the community with his arguments, although (with bitter irony) he is working out his weaknesses.

The letters to the Corinthians are authentic letters (or collections of letters). In 1 Corinthians the letter form is expanded by texts from liturgical contexts. It begins with a short sermon, the 'word of the cross' (1.18 – 4.6). It contains admonitions of the kind that Paul may have also uttered in worship. He quotes the solemn words of the institution of the Lord's Supper. In it Paul strikes up a hymn to love. The letter form is expanded liturgically. It is no coincidence that 1 Corinthians ends with the liturgical formula, 'If anyone has no love for the Lord, let him be accursed. Marana tha – Our Lord, come' (16.22), a formula similar to one which we find

in the eucharistic liturgy of the Didache (Did. 10.6). Whereas
1 Corinthians is a letter expanded liturgically, 2 Corinthians,
like Galatians, is a letter expanded rhetorically. Attempts have
even been made to find the traditions of the Socratic apology
in chs 10 – 13. Both letters aim at leading and directing the
community.

The idea of giving the communities a basis for their life
through the letters of Paul must in fact have been stimulated
by the correspondence with the Corinthians. Even when the
Corinthians were in a deep dispute with Paul, they recognized
the power of his letters: 'For they say his letters are weighty
and strong . . . ' (2 Cor. 10.10). This praise certainly helped
Paul to discover himself as a letter writer. He was urged on to
write the letter in which he crossed the threshold of occasional
writing to become a real author, namely the letter to the
Romans. It is also conceivable that in Corinth he (or followers)
rearranged and edited the letters to the Corinthians. For if
2 Corinthians is a collection of fragments, it could probably have been found acceptable only if the authority of Paul
(or an early circle of editors of his letters) stood behind it.
None of the letters which found their way into 2 Corinthians
have been preserved. Only in Corinth were they all present.
And only in Corinth did people have a motive for working
over the correspondence from the time of crisis and in some
cases deleting remarks which were unacceptable to the
community. So it could be that in Corinth Paul had a second,
equally long 2 Corinthians composed on the model of the
long 1 Corinthians, or that one of his followers did this. At all
events, in Corinth he himself created the great synthesis of
his thought, the letter to the Romans.

## The theological synthesis: Romans as Paul's testament

The letter to the Romans is a treatise in the form of a letter.
From the start it must have been destined to be sent to other
places than Rome. One copy was even intended for Corinth.
For at many points in Romans Paul continues the dialogue
with the Corinthians. Another copy was probably destined

for the community in Ephesus. In this copy Paul expands Romans with a sixteenth chapter specially addressed to the community in Ephesus. In it he sends greetings to Priscilla and Aquila (Rom. 16.3), who were in Ephesus at the time of the Corinthian correspondence (Acts 18.26), and also to Epaenetus, the first convert of the province of 'Asia' with its capital in Ephesus (Rom. 16.5). In this chapter he warns the community in Ephesus entrusted to him about people who are contradicting the doctrine that they had learned. He can do this much more credibly in their case than with the community in Rome, who are strangers to him – indeed he cannot even know what doctrine they had received at the beginning (16.17). Therefore there is much to be said for the old conjecture that Romans 16 was part of a copy of Romans destined for Ephesus. A letter which a priori is destined for several collective addresses is a work of literature.

Nevertheless it is a real letter, which belongs in a concrete situation. There were factors in the situation which compelled Paul to give a systematic summary of his controversial teaching. Paul plans to hand over the collection from the Gentile Christians in Jerusalem and to conclude his mission in the East; after that he wants to go to Rome (15.25–29) and to carry on a mission in Spain from there (15.24). For this he needs the support of the Roman community. So he has to gain their trust. He was not an unknown factor there. In Rome his name was probably associated with the disturbances which had led to the edict of Claudius and the expulsion of many Jewish Christians from Rome. For he was an exponent of that current which was ready to deviate from the traditions of the fathers and to become involved in conflicts as a result. And in doing this he went against the religious policy of Claudius. During Claudius's lifetime Paul had therefore had to abandon his plan to go to Rome (cf. Rom. 1.13). Now (after Claudius's death in AD 54) he wants to realize it. Not everyone in Rome will have been enthusiastic that the notorious troublemaker Paul would be making an appearance there of all places. Paul himself expects to find caricatures of his theology in Rome. There are three central accusations against him. (1) His libertinism teaches people to do evil so that good may come of it (Rom. 3.8). (2) His anti-Judaism challenges the positive special role of Israel (Rom. 3.1ff.). (3) His anti-traditionalism is a political and ecclesiastical risk. Wouldn't his radical teaching once again provoke the intervention of the state against the Christians? And wouldn't it split the communities? Romans is a diplomatic masterpiece, aimed at gaining trust for him and his cause in the face of such accusations against him.

In the first long main part (1.18 – 8.39) Paul develops his doctrine of justification to refute the charge of libertinism which is being levelled against him (esp. 6.1ff.). He makes it clear that his criticism of the law is in no way an invitation to lawless action. The Christian has died to his old being in baptism. He can no longer want to sin. It is absurd to say that Paul invites people to do evil because God forgives! At the same time his criticism of the law is differentiated. Paul emphasizes that 'the law is holy, and the commandment is holy, just and good' (7.12). Only in the hands of human sin does it become a pernicious power. It is a deeply ambivalent power. As 'spirit' it is a power for life, as 'letter' a power for death (7.6 with 2 Cor. 3.6). Whereas negative and positive statements stand directly side by side in Galatians, in Romans Paul can sum up this ambivalence in terms of the letter that kills and the spirit that brings life. This contrast occurred for the first time in 2 Cor. 3.6, but was still absent from Galatians. Here Paul is formulating one of his deepest insights: human beings can pervert any normative system, however holy, into a destructive killing power.

But what about the charge of anti-Judaism? Mustn't he set Jews against him if he takes the offensive in fighting against their identity markers, like circumcision? Paul answers this charge of anti-Judaism in the second part of Romans in three chapters about Israel (Rom. 9 – 11), the content of which is very difficult. He shows that despite all the conflicts between him and other Jews his heart is attached to Israel. He is convinced that in the end all Israel will be saved (11.26); here he clearly qualifies his remark in 1 Thess. 2.16 that the wrath of God has finally come upon the Jews. Here Paul is expressing the hope that the logia source was expressing around the same time (Luke 13.35). In the first generation a final break between Jews and Christians had not yet come about. But on what does Paul now base this belief in the deliverance of Israel? In Rom. 9 – 11 God appears as being so sovereign that he can elect people even without faith. Paul experienced that himself. As an enemy of the Christians he had been converted and saved by an appearance from heaven – at a time when he was still an unbeliever. Now he hopes that God will also save Israel, which continues to be hostile to Christianity, by such an appearance of Jesus from heaven (namely through his coming at the parousia). For many theologians this statement that all Jews will be saved, by-passing the church but not without encountering Christ, is so bold that they cannot credit Paul with it. But that is the most probable interpretation of Rom. 11.26.

Finally there was the fear that it would be a political risk. So in the last 'paraenetic' part of Romans (12.1 – 15.13) Paul emphasizes his absolute political loyalty (13.1–7), on the one hand with the argument deriving from the Jewish tradition that God has given their power to those who hold power (here he omits the notion that God takes power from unjust authorities); and on the other hand with the notion deriving from the Greek tradition that the state must further the good and fight evil (here he omits the notion that one can distinguish between tyrants and kings). Rather, he formulates an apodeictic prohibition against resisting the state. Such an apostle cannot represent a political risk. So before we criticize Rom. 13.1ff. as an uncritical ethic of submission we should reflect that Paul is admonishing his readers to be subject to the *exousiai*, i.e. the officials in the Roman empire. Here the term *exousia* always means constitutional authority. It is also striking that in a letter to the Romans he suppresses the fact that the emperor stands at the head of all 'offices'. Did Paul know that the emperor's authority rested only on a combination of legitimate republican authorities? In that case we could understand Rom. 13.1ff. as an expression of a legitimistic attitude which recognizes only constitutional rule, and not the arbitrary rule of an individual.

Paul has a second problem. Even if he represents no danger to the external relations of the community, he could split the communities internally. Paul has to assume that the way in which he put the unity of the community at risk over the food regulations by remaining deeply faithful to principles (or being stubborn) in the conflict in Antioch has become known. So he uses the example of the strong and the weak, i.e. Christians who eat everything and vegetarians, who in principle eat no meat, to explain that he can resolve such conflicts by a social agreement. In Rom. 14.1 – 15.13 he admonishes the two groups to tolerate each other in the community; however, the strong are to adapt to the weak and renounce their rights, rather than the weak doing anything that goes against their conviction.

Romans is the mature summary of Pauline theology. In terms of content it combines the yield of the letters against the Judaizers and those against the enthusiasts and retracts exaggerated formulations from these sometimes very polemical letters. Formally, too, we have a synthesis here: the structure of Romans is based on the anti-Judaizing Galatians, into which important sections are inserted from the anti-enthusiastic 1 Corinthians. I can only give a brief sketch of the two here.

Galatians and Romans develop Paul's teaching on justification, both by applying the example of Abraham twice: in Gal. 3.1 – 4.6 Abraham is the father of a unity which overcomes all social barriers; in 4.21ff. he is the father of two hostile descendants. Likewise in Rom. 4.1ff. Abraham is the forefather of all believers from Jews and Gentiles, while in 9.6ff. he is the forefather of an Israel torn apart by a split. The two main parts of Romans follow the structure of Galatians. This is continued in the paraenetic closing part. For here in both letters the command to love one's neighbour stands at the centre as a summary of the commandments (Gal. 5.14; Rom. 13.9). However, in Galatians we do not detect any hope of overcoming the opposition between Jews and Christians as two different children of Abraham. Enmity between them continues. But in Romans Paul struggles through to a belief in the redemption of all Israel (Rom. 11.26). Judaism and the law are evaluated more positively in Romans than in Galatians. Formally Romans may follow Galatians, but in content it withdraws this anti-Judaistic tendency.

Now parts of 1 Corinthians have been inserted into the structure of Romans which comes from Galatians: the Adam–Christ typology in Rom. 5.12–21, the discussion of baptism in Rom. 6.1ff., the image of the body of Christ in Rom. 12.3ff. and the discussion about strength and weakness in Rom. 14.1ff. Paul uses the resumption of these themes to carry on his conversation with the Corinthians. It is striking that, for example, the theme of the Spirit fades into the background. In 1 Corinthians the Adam–Christ typology emphasizes the opposition between the psychic and the pneumatic person (1 Cor. 15.45ff.); baptism is the bestowal of the Spirit (6.11) and the image of the body of Christ is thought of in terms of the pneuma, in so far as the spirit gives the body its unity (12.13). By contrast, in Romans Paul discusses these themes in a very much more 'sober' way: in Rom. 5.12ff., in contrast to Adam Christ is the obedient man, not the pneumatic man. In Rom. 6.1ff. baptism is dying with Christ; the Spirit is not mentioned. In Rom. 12.3ff. the body of Christ is formed not through the Spirit but through mutual services. We can detect a correction to the Corinthian enthusiasm. And not only that, in Rom. 8 this enthusiasm is reinterpreted in a convincing way: here the Spirit is the power of the new life and the expression of a deep bond with all suffering in the world – as an inexpressible sigh from the depths, in which the sigh of creatures is articulated. But at the same time Paul establishes a bond with Christ on high: just as the Spirit enters the depths of the human heart, so Christ enters before God (cf. Rom. 8.27 with 8.34). Here Paul sketches out a theology of the Spirit which surpasses all that he has said previously about the Spirit. In so doing he evaluates the pneumatic experience of the Corinthians positively and in quite a new way. All this is also a message to the community in Corinth, which in Romans is always kept in view as one of the audiences being addressed. We may in fact begin by assuming that what Paul wrote in Romans he will also have argued by word of mouth in Corinth. It could also have become known through his scribe Tertius

(Rom. 16.22) or through a copy of Romans in the community. And it was Paul's wish that it should be made known in the community.

Just as Paul retracts the anti-Judaistic tendency of Galatians in Romans, so too he retracts the anti-enthusiastic tendency of 1 Corinthians. He arrives at a positive synthesis: in Galatians he had played off the Spirit against the law; in Romans he calls the law itself 'spiritual' (7.14). In 1 Corinthians he had played off love against the irrational dynamic of the Spirit; in Romans the Spirit itself fills human hearts with the love of God (Rom. 5.5). The functions of both the law and the Spirit are redefined and the two are reconciled, so that Paul can speak of the 'law of the Spirit and life' (Rom. 8.2). The opposition between nomism and enthusiasm has been overcome.

The letter form is expanded into a treatise in letter form in Romans largely because Paul takes up and reformulates notions from earlier letters. This makes Romans what Günther Bornkamm has called 'Paul's testament'. That is true of both its content and its form.

In it Paul has inserted his doctrine of justification into the religious and cultural information of history. This doctrine says that God attributes to all men and women the same value and lack of value regardless of their origin. All have an infinite value, contrary to the facts of their actual life, because it is God's will to create all anew as creatures through Christ and to reconcile them with himself. God himself will bring that about through cross and resurrection. Here human beings can no more create themselves anew than they created themselves at their birth. Therefore here human actions cannot achieve anything. This radical relativization of human actions for salvation began with the discussion of apparently external ritual actions, but in Romans Paul extends it to all ethical actions. Human actions are unimportant for redemption through God, but they are decisive for the ethical treatment of others. The person who is transformed creatively by God's Spirit does good spontaneously. This is a consequence of his or her deliverance, but not the condition for it. The success of a person's life is based solely on trust in that internal transformation by dying and rising again with Christ which make human beings new creatures. The relativization of human actions (or works) was so strong in Paul that he was not interested even in the earthly actions and works of the man Jesus.

But we must not see the point of this doctrine of justification only in the relationship between human beings and God. Paul's extreme religion of grace represented a consistent relativization of the social and cultural boundaries between human beings – an opening up of the Jewish religion to everyone. The core issue was that if all human beings are by nature equally remote from God, they are much closer to one another than they think that they are. If God treats them all equally with his offer of salvation, then inequalities are only 'human'. In Paul a universalistic tendency of the Jewish religion breaks through. His heart opens up when, using an already-existing formula, he writes: 'There is no longer Jew nor Greek, slave nor free, male nor female, for you are all one in Christ Jesus' (Gal. 3.28).

But Romans is also 'Paul's testament' in a formal sense. The theology developed here is rooted in Paul's biography, the result of his whole life. But he formulated it clearly only in controversy with the Judaizers. The historical result was the failure of the attempt to reincorporate the Christian groups into Judaism by adopting circumcision and food regulations. Now in Romans Paul wanted to ensure that this openness of Jewish faith remained permanent for all men and women – even beyond his possible death. So we can also call Romans a 'testament' in the formal sense. Paul reckoned with the possibility of his death in Judaea (Rom. 15.31). He knew that he had to leave the East and the communities which he had founded, and suspected that this would be goodbye for ever. In this situation, he wants to put his followers in the position of being able to carry on his message independently of him by means of a written summary of his theology. His intimations were not unfounded. As he had announced in Romans, he set off for Jerusalem with a delegation from his communities and the collection made from them; he was arrested as an apostate and religious troublemaker, was taken to Rome after a two-year imprisonment in Caesarea, and died there around AD 60.

In a short period – between around 51 and 56 – Paul developed the community letter from an occasional writing into a literary form which in his case already called for publication. Granted, Romans is still a proper letter addressed to specific readers (and many incidental readers). But it already displays features of a public letter. Such public letters were familiar to the inhabitants of the Roman empire as edicts of emperors and governors. They were often chiselled on inscriptions so that everyone could read them. At the beginning the sender identified himself, with all his titles. The Gallio inscription in Delphi mentioned above (if we fill out the abbreviations and gaps in the fragmentary tradition) begins: 'Tiberius Claudius Caesar Augustus Germanicus, in the twelfth year of his tribunate, proclaimed emperor for the twenty-sixth time, father of the fatherland, greets . . .' In Romans, Paul too introduces himself with resounding titles. He had not done this in any previous letter. He emphasizes that he is acting on behalf of a ruler of the world and that his mission concerns all peoples:

> Paul, a servant of Jesus Christ, called to be an apostle, set apart from the gospel of God, which he promised beforehand through his prophets in the holy scriptures, the gospel concerning his son, who was descended from David according to the flesh and designated Son of God in power according to the Spirit of holiness by his resurrection from the dead, Jesus Christ our Lord, through whom we have received grace and apostleship to bring about the obedience of faith for the sake of his name among all the nations, including yourselves who are called to belong to Jesus Christ. (Rom. 1.1–6)

People in the provinces were familiar with letters from Rome with such resounding official titles. Here, however, someone is writing from the provinces to Rome; it is true that he is addressing only the Christians in Rome, but they represent all individuals and peoples. Paul cannot make the public claim of his message and his writing clearer. There were no forms of language for the public message of a 'private man' to the whole world. So Paul slips into the language of political edicts. He speaks in the name of a king from the house of David who has become world ruler over all peoples by his resurrection. Here he could be deliberately alluding to the emperor. For when he speaks of Christ as a royal son from the house of David who has really (i.e. in power) been nominated Son of God by resurrection from the dead, this is perhaps a deliberate counter-image to the emperor Claudius, about whose apotheosis after his death Seneca was circulating a mordant satire in Rome at the time.

In the letters of Paul we leave the rural areas of Galilee and enter the great world of the Mediterranean cities. It is a different world from that of the Jesus traditions in the synoptic gospels. The radius has become greater, but the content more moderate. In Paul the radicalism of the itinerant charismatics has given way to an orientation on the needs of sedentary communities. His ethic is more moderate. Only after his death did the second basic literary form of primitive Christianity, the gospel, arise, which has preserved for us the Jesus traditions of the itinerant charismatics and the first local communities. Despite their radicalism, these traditions were handed on for long enough in oral tradition to remain preserved in writing for all times. How did that come about? And why was there initially such a delay?

# CHAPTER 6

# The Synoptic Gospels and the Acts of the Apostles: The New Form of Literature in the Second and Third Generations

In the first generation itinerant apostles were the great authorities in primitive Christianity. In Palestine and Syria they went from village to village, handed on the sayings of Jesus and continued the form of his life. Local settled groups of sympathizers supported them. Often only 'two or three' of them would meet together (Matt. 18.20). The logia source collected their traditions in a prophetic book in which Jesus appeared as the one who surpassed all the prophets. By contrast, in Asia Minor and the Aegean missionaries like Paul appeared. They travelled from city to city (also by ship) and worked in order to be able to finance their travels. Paul, the greatest of them, founded communities which grew rapidly, and he discovered that at an early stage they wanted a degree of independence from their founders. Here, in the Aegean, the community letter came into being, in which Jesus is depicted as a mythical being. It was not the earthly Jesus but the apostle Paul's preaching of Christ that was the decisive authority here. The situation changed in the second generation. (1) The first generation and the apostles died out. (2) The local communities grew stronger. (3) The Jerusalem temple was destroyed. (4) The importance of the Gentile Christians increased. All this contributed to the formation of the gospels.

1.  Paul, Peter and James were executed between AD 60 and AD 64. This caused a gap in authority. To fill it, people within the sphere of the primitive Christian letter literature wrote letters in the name of the dead apostles. Primitive Christian pseudepigraphy filled the gap in authority. For the 'Deutero-Pauline' letters 'the apostle' is the decisive authority, whereas sayings of Jesus are quoted even less in them than they are by Paul. In the sphere of the Jesus tradition, however, people reactivated the authority of the earthly Jesus. The gap in authority which had come about with the death of the apostles thus provided the impulse to elevate the authority of Jesus in literary form in gospels. In them there was a desire to bring together what was to govern the life of the communities. Whereas the primitive Christian letters were intended to guide the communities directly, the gospels exercised authority indirectly, in that they told of the life of Jesus.

2.  With the departure of the great authorities the influence of all the itinerant charismatics declined. The local communities which they had founded increased in importance. The disciples' tradition of itinerant radicalism had already taken literary form in the logia source; the traditions of the community and the people now first took form in the gospels. In them traditions of the local communities were also collected alongside traditions of the itinerant charismatics. And not only that. These traditions (like the passion story) gave the gospels their form. As Martin Kähler put it, they are 'passion narratives with an extended introduction'. They preface the passion story with the synoptic apocalypse as a further community tradition. The previous narrative is shaped towards this end. Here the earliest gospel uses the internal structure of the miracle stories:

these work towards a confession of the miracle-worker, which in Mark is delayed time and again until it is pronounced by the centurion under the cross. The Gospel of Mark still found miracle stories as living popular tradition. The evangelist himself gives an indication of this when he says that the miracles of Jesus are being related everywhere – even against Jesus' will (i.e. beyond the control of the Christian community, Mark 7.36). He has reintegrated this free Jesus tradition into the community tradition. In its structure the earliest gospel is clearly governed more strongly by traditions from the community and the people than by traditions of the disciples on which itinerant charismatics have left their traces. We shall see that it revises these traditions of the disciples in such a way that they are also accessible to Christians in local communities.

3. The earliest gospel grapples intensively with the destruction of the Jerusalem temple in AD 70. With it the bond which held Jews and Christians together disappeared. Granted, only the Jewish Christians had taken part in temple worship. But there was a lively hope that one day the Gentile Christians would also be admitted. Jesus still prophesies in the Gospel of Mark that the temple will become 'a house of prayer for all peoples' (11.17). After its loss as the centre of the Jewish ritual system the Christians had to reflect on their own rites and push ahead with the transition from a religion of the temple to a religion of the book, which Judaism was also making at the same time. But as yet there was no book which contained the essential narrative of the Christians as the basis of their ethic and their rite. The logia source provided no foundation for either baptism or the Lord's Supper, nor did it explain why Christianity had developed into an independent religion alongside Judaism. Here the Gospel of Mark helped. It depicts the conflict between Jesus and his Jewish contemporaries. The main point of dispute consists in ritual questions like the commandments about the sabbath

and cleanness. It sets new Christian rites over against the ritual norms of Judaism. The Gospel of Mark surrounds the two focal points of the 'baptism of Jesus' at the beginning and the 'Lord's Supper' at the end like an ellipse. After the loss of the temple as the centre of the Jewish ritual system it provides the basis for the rites of the Christian community in a new key narrative with which the Christians finally take leave of the narrative community of Judaism.

4. With the destruction of the temple the separation from Judaism was final, and Gentile Christianity gained importance. Perhaps it was only now that some Jewish-Christian communities opened themselves up to Gentiles. Thus in the parable of the marriage feast (Matt. 22.1ff.), the invitation goes out to all – including the Gentiles – only after the destruction of Jerusalem. The change to a Gentile audience encouraged a trend to develop the Jewish form of the prophetic book (as we have it in Q) into a Hellenistic *bios*. In the non-Jewish milieu there was nothing strange about concentrating a literary genre on a person. So it is no coincidence that all the gospels were written for communities with Gentile Christians. Their place of origin is Syria, the birthplace of the mission to the Gentiles. There (and hardly in Rome) 'Mark' wrote the first gospel. There Matthew expanded it by the logia source. Only Luke developed the gospel form fundamentally further, creating a balance between the authority of Jesus (in his gospel) and the influence of the apostles (in Acts). He did not write in Syria. He was certainly familiar with the world of the Mediterranean cities in the West, in which the authority of the apostle was decisive.

These four factors are not independent of one another. They were all governed by a great political crisis. In the late 50s and 60s the tensions between Jews and Romans grew in Palestine, so that in 66 there was a rebellion of the Jews against the Romans, in which in AD 70 the temple was destroyed. The tensions before this rebellion contributed to the martyr deaths of the most important authorities of primitive Christianity. The fundamentalist zeal of the Jews was Paul's undoing when he was arrested in Jerusalem around AD 58. He could also have been executed in Rome because it was thought there that trouble-makers in Palestine had to be dealt with harshly. James fell victim to internal conflicts in Judaism. His opponent was the Sadducean high priest Ananus, who led the first phase of the rebellion against the Romans. The Jewish war changed relations between Jews and Christians. The temple which hitherto they had shared was lost. But it also altered the relationship between Jewish Christians and Gentile Christians. Palestinian Jewish Christianity was weakened by this war and Gentile Christianity was strengthened. Now Palestinian Jewish Christianity together with the neighbouring regions of Syria was the home of the itinerant charismatics. Their importance also declined with the declining importance of Palestine. So we can say that just as the rise of the New Testament letter literature is to be seen against the background of the religious policy of Claudius, so the origin of the gospel literature is to be seen against the background of the Jewish war. The letter literature came into being as an instrument for guiding the community in the Judaistic crisis. The gospel literature came into being out of the need to reorientate the communities after the Jewish war.

In addition, however, there is a central theological motive which underlies the formation of the gospels, but which also delayed it. In the monotheistic milieu of Jewish Christianity it was impossible to write a *bios* of Jesus in which there was even the slightest indication that on the basis of his own words and works Jesus had claimed to be God or Son of God. That would have been blasphemy. Only God himself could bestow and reveal this dignity (cf. Luke 10.22). The worship of Jesus as 'Son of God' was grounded solely in the cross and Easter, i.e. in an action of God towards Jesus. The problem was: how could one relate actions and sayings of Jesus without giving the impression that he divinized himself in his lifetime? This problem can be detected above all in the earliest gospel. The Gospel of Mark could surround the whole earthly life of Jesus with a divine aura because it was addressed to Gentile

Christians who had no reservations about the appearance of a deity in human form. But this divine aura had to be shrouded in mystery, because the gospel was also speaking to Jewish Christians who could accept this radiance only as the splendour of the creator God who overcomes death, i.e. only on the basis of the Easter appearances. The Markan messianic secret is a literary form given to the 'monotheistic' reservations about a life of Jesus bathed in the divine splendour. The need for a picture of Jesus which gave the community a new orientation after the great crisis of the Jewish war won through in the face of this reservation. And it is the achievement of Mark the evangelist that he did not simply mask this reservation but shaped it in a convincing way.

## The Gospel of Mark

The Gospel of Mark was written shortly after AD 70. The destruction of the temple is presupposed. Jesus prophesies it in Mark 13.1–2 as if it has in fact taken place. Before the Sanhedrin he is confronted with an altered version of his prophecy as false testimony: he is said to have announced that he will destroy the temple (in the singular!) and rebuild it in three days (14.58). However, it was not Jesus but the Romans who destroyed all the buildings in the temple precinct, leaving the temple platform standing. No new temple was built. Now readers still have 13.1–2 ringing in their ears. There Jesus proclaims that all the 'great buildings' (in the plural) and not just the temple proper (in the singular) will be destroyed. Their destruction is spoken of in the passive. Who brings it about is left open, so that it could also be the Romans. Thus Jesus' saying corresponds to reality precisely where the false statement contradicts it. If (like the evangelist himself) we regard 13.1–2 as a correction of 14.58, it would be a correction which adapts Jesus' saying to actual events. But in that case the temple would already be destroyed. Nevertheless some exegetes think that Mark still expected the destruction of the temple and was writing shortly before AD 70.

Mark was written in Syria. Admittedly, the tradition of the early church says that it was written in Rome, and that its author was the 'John Mark' from Jerusalem who in 1 Peter 5.13 is associated with Rome (= Babylon), but was also highly regarded in Syria. However, the information about Palestine is too full of mistakes to come from a former inhabitant of Jerusalem. According to Mark 5.1ff., Gerasa lies on Lake Gennesaret, but in fact it is more than thirty miles south of there. However, the author cannot live very far away from Palestine either. He has contact with oral Jesus tradition of the kind that was more likely to have circulated in the neighbourhood of Palestine than in distant Rome. He roots Jesus in a rural world which is also his own. For him Lake Gennesaret is a 'lake', and not a 'sea' as it is for Luke, with his experience of the world. Something else that tells against Rome is that he equates the smallest coin in Rome, the quadrans, with two even smaller coins, and in the East these were coined only by Herod (cf. the literal translation of Mark 12.42).

Mark writes above all for Gentile Christians. The culminating point of his gospel is that a Gentile centurion is the first person to recognize Jesus as a 'Son of God' (15.39). The mission to all the Gentiles is the great task before the end of the world (13.10). The explanation of Jewish customs also fits Gentile-Christian readers (7.3–4).

The secret about Jesus about which the reader is enlightened right at the beginning is characteristic of Mark: John the Baptist announces one who is '*stronger*' and is confirmed and surpassed by the voice of God, which addresses Jesus as the 'beloved *Son*' in the second person singular (1.9–11). Here Jesus is adopted as Son of God (and not just identified as such). By having the spirit bestowed on him at baptism he has just undergone a change of status. And all Christians knew from their own experience that the spirit bestowed a new status and did not just confirm an already existing dignity. They had to understand the voice at Jesus' baptism in precisely the same way. It is interesting that in the Gospel of Mark all these events are depicted as a subjective experience of Jesus. The other persons in the text do not notice anything. For a long time only demons with supernatural knowledge know who Jesus is (Mark 1.24; 1.34; 3.11), whereas the disciples do not understand him (4.41; 6.52; 8.21ff.). Therefore Jesus forbids the demons to speak of him and tries to get his disciples to understand – for a long time without success.

The mystery of his person is resolved only in the middle of the gospel. After the healing of a blind man with symbolic significance – the eyes of the disciples who are blind to Jesus' dignity are opened – Peter confesses for all the disciples that Jesus is the '*Messiah*' (8.29). But he protests against the journey to suffering in Jerusalem and is sharply rebuked for this (8.33). Sayings follow which call to discipleship in suffering. Only after that is the true dignity of Jesus unveiled to some disciples. At the transfiguration on the mountain the three closest disciples see Jesus' glory (9.2–10). A voice from heaven again corrects the human expectations which have been expressed previously. It addresses the disciples directly and says of Jesus in the third person, 'That is my beloved *Son*, hear him!' The Son of God is introduced. But all the disciples are to be silent about him 'until the Son of Man is risen from the dead' (9.9).

Finally, at the end, a Gentile centurion recognizes immediately after Jesus' death, 'Truly, this man was God's son' (15.39). This time an angel who has come from heaven corrects his statement by proclaiming the primitive Christian Easter message at the tomb: the dead man *was* not God's son. 'He *is* risen' (16.6). God has won the victory over death. Only after Easter can the disciples openly proclaim Jesus the Son of God. But that is not part of the narrative.

So heaven opens three times in the Gospel of Mark. God's voice and his messenger speak into the human world and disclose successively who Jesus is. They always take up human expectations, surpass them and correct them. People may have an inkling of who Jesus is, but his true being is known only on the basis of a self-revelation of God – perhaps in three deliberate stages: adoption (1.11), presentation (9.7) and his acceptance into God's world, which remains surrounded with mystery. These three 'epiphanies' provide the structure of the Gospel of Mark. At its centre are the confession of Peter and the transfiguration. Before this, Jesus is active in Galilee and its surroundings, and then his way to suffering in Jerusalem begins. Previously his disciples do not understand his dignity, but afterwards they do not understand the lowliness of his suffering.

Why does Mark veil the dignity of Jesus during his lifetime so much with mystery and misunderstanding? By the successive unveiling of the mystery he not only creates a narrative tension, but also expresses a monotheistic reservation. This can be made clear by a comparison between Jesus in the Gospel of Mark and Herod Agrippa I in Acts. When Agrippa does not reject the homage paid to him as a god, he is punished with death because of his self-apotheosis (Acts 12.19–23). By contrast Jesus rejects any deification by human beings. When demons call him 'Son of God', he abruptly rejects them. Only 'possessed' people can do something like this. Bestowing a high status on Jesus and revealing his true being is God's concern alone. Mark also expresses that positively. In 12.29 Jesus utters the monotheistic confession of Israel, 'Hear, Israel, the Lord our God is the only Lord.' A scribe agrees: 'He alone is the Lord and there is none other beside him' (12.32). But by the time of Mark Christians had already long been worshipping Jesus as their 'Lord' alongside God. So immediately afterwards, Ps. 110.1 is quoted in the Gospel of Mark: 'The Lord said to my Lord (= Jesus): sit at my right hand, and I will put your enemies under your feet' (12.36). The only 'Lord' there can be alongside the one God is the Lord whom God himself has exalted to that status. And that happens in the resurrection of the crucified Jesus.

Now if only the cross and resurrection can be the substantive basis of the divine dignity of Jesus, we can understand why they must remain a secret until that point. Therefore the traditional interpretation of the 'messianic secret' is right: in the Gospel of Mark the worship of Jesus as Son of God which was originally bound up with his resurrection is projected back on to the life of Jesus. As William Wrede recognized, Jesus was the Son of God, but he was so secretly. Certainly Jesus was proclaimed Son of God as early as at his baptism, but he and those around him had to wait for God's decisive action to be able to confess him Son of God. They thus warded off the suspicion that Jesus had arrogantly claimed divine status. That would be blasphemy (2.6–7; 14.64). Only God can bestow that on him. We can still see in Mark how there are scruples about projecting the divinity of Jesus back on to the earthly life of Jesus.

However, precisely because of this, in the Gospel of Mark Jesus is bathed in a mysterious aura – as if he were an unknown God walking on the earth. At one point he exclaims, 'How long must I still be with you?' (9.19). With him God comes near to human beings – not in exalted majesty but as a man who ends on the cross. His followers are bound up with him through suffering: after Peter's messianic confession and the first prediction of the passion he demands of the disciples, 'Whoever will be my disciple, let him deny himself, take up his cross and follow me' (8.34). Then they will also see his glory, which is revealed to the three closest disciples on the mountain only after this exclamation. Here Mark is addressing communities which are being persecuted (13.9–13). He not only requires them to be hard on themselves but also gives them some pragmatic support in their lives. If initially Jesus himself kept his identity secret, so too his disciples may with good consciences keep secret their identity as Christians. They need not leave the protection of the secret unnecessarily. One day their identity will inevitably be confessed, as Jesus was confessed. The moment is coming when they will stand before their judges and confess that they are Christians – as Jesus confessed his identity as messiah before his judges (14.61–62). In initially wanting to remain secret, the Son of God gives his followers a good conscience: they need not enter the public arena unnecessarily and risk conflicts.

But the notion of discipleship is illuminating in yet another respect. 'Discipleship' originally meant the homeless life of itinerant charismatics. Mark extends the term so that it also covers local communities. One of the first people whom Jesus calls to discipleship is the toll collector Levi (2.13–17). Levi invites Jesus into his house and holds a feast there. He is absent from the list of the twelve disciples who are always to be with Jesus (3.13–19). By this Mark indicates that he remained in his home. He is to be a figure with whom members of the local communities who did not share the itinerant life of Jesus can identify. When many accept Jesus' invitation to 'follow' him at this feast, 'following' him, 'discipleship', becomes a matter of taking part in the meals which were part of the life of each local community. There is a further extension of the concept of discipleship at the middle and at the end of the gospel: here discipleship is also defined as readiness for suffering (8.34–35) and loving care (15.41). These two qualities could be required of both itinerant charismatics and of local communities. So we can say that the logia source brings together the disciple traditions of the itinerant charismatics. By contrast, Mark brings together the traditions of the local communities and works traditions of the itinerant charismatics into them (like the notion of discipleship), so that these become accessible to all Christians.

In Mark, the disciples prove to have no understanding and to be blind in their discipleship. They understand neither Jesus' lofty status in his miracles (6.52) nor his lowliness in suffering (8.32–33; 10.32). They understand neither the miracle stories nor the passion story – the two groups of texts which are (largely) lacking in the logia source. In the persons of the disciples who do not understand is there perhaps criticism of itinerant charismatics of the type standing behind the logia source? That is uncertain. At all events, though, the disciples who do not understand provide the background for the true understanding of Jesus to which Mark wants to lead his readers.

But who are the readers to understand Jesus to be? Jesus is the royal messiah, whose accession to power is proclaimed as 'gospel'. Already before Mark the term 'gospel' denoted proclamation *about* Jesus (cf. 1 Cor. 15.1ff.; Rom. 1.3–4). Mark introduces it into the Jesus tradition (1.1; 14.9) and extends it to the preaching of Jesus (1.14). For him, what Jesus did and taught is just as much 'gospel' as what God has done to him in cross and resurrection. In his case, 'gospel' also takes on an additional meaning. There is evidence of the noun 'gospel' (in contrast to the verb 'evangelize') above all in the emperor ideology. 'Gospels' (in the plural) denote the good news of the birth, the accession or the victory of the emperor.

Such 'gospels' were celebrated during the time of Mark in Syria and elsewhere as news of the proclamation of Vespasian as emperor in AD 58 (*War,* 4, 618; cf. *War,* 4, 656–57). So we can ask whether Mark deliberately termed the content of his description of Jesus 'gospel' because he understood it as an 'anti-gospel' to the rise of the Flavians. Was the point of his gospel that the Christians should not bow before the Roman emperor, but that the centurion, as the representative of the world power of Rome, should bow before the crucified Jesus?

## The Gospel of Matthew

The evangelist Matthew also wrote in Syria. There are the following indications of this. He calls Jesus a 'Nazorean' (2.23), the name given to the Christians there. He has the reputation of Jesus spreading as far as 'Syria' (4.24). There his gospel is quoted in IgnSm. 1.1 and in the Didache. It was therefore written around AD 80–100, before the letters of Ignatius (before AD 107/110) and after the Gospel of Mark (*c.* AD 75). It does not come from the apostle Matthew, as it is un-imaginable that an eyewitness should have used the Gospel of Mark as a source where he himself was present. It is con-ceivable that one of his sources, the logia source, was attributed to Matthew – and that Matthew's name was transferred to the whole gospel, although it was written by someone else.

The Gospel of Mark and Q are the sources of the Gospel of Matthew. He could have come across both in his time in Syria. The Gospel of Mark was composed there, and the logia source was perhaps brought there by emigrants from Palestine. The evangelist Matthew is at home in the Jewish-Christian theology of the logia source. The mere structure of his book, with its five discourses, shows that he attaches decisive importance to the sayings of Jesus. Here he corrects some Jewish-Christian one-sidedness, for example when he makes the Risen Christ do away with the limitation of the mission to Israel indicated in 10.5–6 (28.19–20). But he also corrects the Gentile-Christian Gospel of Mark, which had declared all foods clean. But Matthew omits this particular remark, made in Mark 7.19 (cf. Matt. 15.17). If by such corrections the Gospel of Matthew combines a Jewish- and a Gentile-Christian source, it is probable that it also sets out to unite Jewish and Gentile Christians in reality. We shall consider what each of his two sources prompted him to do.

The logia source inspired Matthew to structure his gospel by five discourses. Each is to some degree a little 'logia source': the Sermon on the Mount at the beginning, the mission, parable and community discourses in the middle and the eschatological discourse at the end (Matt. 5 – 7; 10; 13; 18; 23 – 25). Matthew characterizes them each time by a closing formula: 'When Jesus had ended this discourse . . .' (7.28, etc.). The disciples are to disseminate Jesus' teaching in these discourses throughout the world so that all peoples 'obey what I have commanded you' (28.20). He sums up his special concern in four formulations which become increasingly complex in structure.

1.  He sums up the most important content of the Sermon on the Mount in *one* sentence: 'So whatever you wish that men would do to you, do so to them; for this is the law and the prophets' (7.12).

2.  A second summary is the *twofold commandment* to love: 'You shall love the Lord your God with all your heart, and with all your soul, and with all your mind. This is the greatest and first commandment. And a second is like it, You shall love your neighbour as yourself. On these two commandments depend all the law and the prophets' (22.37–40).

3.  He mentions 'the weightier matters of the law' again in 23.23: 'justice and mercy and faith'. These *three* are more important than ritual demands like the tithing of the three cooking herbs mint, dill and cumin.

4.  There is a list of the *six acts of mercy* at the end of Jesus' last discourse. There the judge of the world encounters all men and women. Regardless of whether they are Jews, Christians or Gentiles they are all judged by the standard of whether they have helped the Son of Man

in the least of his brethren. The righteous do not know that they have helped him. Jesus explains to them: 'I was hungry and you gave me food, I was thirsty and you gave me drink, I was a stranger and you welcomed me, I was sick and you visited me, I was in prison and you came to me' (25.35–36). Many exegetes think that such an interpretation in terms of all men and women and all sufferers is too bold. They say that the text measures non-Christians by what they had done to Christians (the brothers of the Son of Man). Perhaps they under-estimate the humane content of Matthew's ethic.

In Matthew we find a consistently ethical Christianity with a Jewish-Christian stamp. The Matthaean Jesus seeks to fulfil the true intention of the Jewish tradition (law and prophets) (5.17). Unlike Paul he does not promise any certainty of salvation. Paul could assure his readers that 'there is therefore now no condemnation for those who are in Christ Jesus' (Rom. 8.1). By contrast, Matthew says, 'Not every one who says to me "Lord, Lord" shall enter the kingdom of heaven, but he who does the will of my Father who is in heaven' (Matt. 7.21). Matthew requires at least a readiness to forgive (Matt. 6.14; 18.23ff.) and an elementary readiness to help by performing acts of mercy as conditions for salvation (Matt. 6.14; 18.23ff.). Anyone can do that. A person does not need to be transformed (as Paul argues) by a miraculous power (like the spirit). It is only Christians with Paul's pessimistic anthropology who think that Matthew's ethical demands ask too much. By contrast, Matthew shares the ethical optimism of the Jewish tradition: man is created to fulfil the law. Even more so are Christians, for whom Jesus interprets the law in a humane way, so that it is no longer a heavy burden (Matt. 11.28–30). God does not require the impossible of anyone. Who has never helped a hungry person? Who has never visited a sick person at least once? And who would be so blind as not to forgive others – when he or she is not perfect!

Matthew proclaims this humane ethic deeply rooted in Judaism as a 'global ethic' that is to bind all peoples together. He deliberately universalizes a particular tradition. Although he has ordinary people in view, he proclaims with an aristocratic claim, 'You are the salt of the earth!', 'You are the light of the world' (5.13, 14). In what situation was this gospel formulated with such tremendous ethical energy? We learn something about that when we look at the way in which Matthew has used his second source.

Matthew puts the discourses in the framework of the Gentile-Christian Gospel of Mark, but expands this framework at the beginning and the end. He prefaces it with stories about Jesus' infancy, which present Jesus as son of David, and adds Easter stories in which Jesus accedes to rule of the world: 'All authority in heaven and on earth has been given to me. So go to all peoples . . .' (28.18–20). Thus Matthew writes a gospel of a Jewish king who rises to be ruler of the world. However, he is a quite special ruler of the world.

- He wants to rule the world not by troops but by words. The 'son of David' is a peaceful king. He pronounces the peacemakers blessed (5.9). He does not fight, but seeks to help right gain the victory (12.18–21). He enters his capital on an ass, as a counter-image to military rulers (21.5).

- He fulfils the expectations of the Jews in a precise way. As the scriptures have prophesied, he comes from Bethlehem, is summoned back out of Egypt, is called a Nazorean and moves to Capernaum (2.6, 15, 23; 4.13, 16). Matthew wants to demonstrate the fulfilment of the Old Testament in those details which have always governed a person's identity: Who are his ancestors? Where does he come from?

- But the expectations of the Gentiles are also fulfilled in this ruler. At his birth three wise men come from the East, representatives of pagan astrology who expect a new king (2.1ff.). On him the Gentiles set their hope (12.21).

All this fits the historical situation after the Jewish war. During the war not only Jews but other peoples in the East were stirred by the expectation that a ruler from the East would attain rule over the world. Josephus knows of an ambiguous oracle that was also in the scriptures of the Jews, according to which someone from their land would attain to world rule; but many wise men had proved wrong in their judgment (*War* 6, 312–13). Josephus himself related the prophecy to Vespasian, who came from the East and rose to be emperor (*War* 3, 351ff.). After the war Matthew is grappling with such expectations. His thesis is that Jesus of Nazareth is this new world ruler from the East, expected by Gentiles and Jews. Therefore he attaches importance to biographical details in order to be able to show that Jesus is this ruler and no other. That is why he introduces him as a Jewish ruler with a long genealogy (1.1–17). That is why he demonstrates by the story of the magicians from the East (2.1ff.) that the expectations of the Gentiles are also fulfilled in him. That is why he transfers to him the motif of the hostility of the old ruler to the new, who as a child only with difficulty escapes the persecutions of the old ruler (2.13ff.). What is decisive for him is that this ruler will rule through his ethical teaching. He interprets the Jewish Torah in such a way that it applies to Gentiles and Jews all over the world.

Whence this confidence? It, too, is connected with the Jewish war. After this catastrophe Rabbi Johanan ben Zakkai founded the school in Jabneh from which a renewal movement came. In the face of the destruction of the temple he comforted his fellow-countrymen with Hos. 6.6, where God says, 'I want mercy, not sacrifice!' Showing mercy can completely replace sacrifice. We find this particular quotation of Hos. 6.6 twice in the Gospel of Matthew, which was composed at the same time (9.13; 12.7). Both times Matthew has inserted it into the text of Mark. The second time (in the story about plucking ears of corn on the sabbath) it refers directly to the temple. It says, 'Here is something that is greater than the temple' – namely mercy (12.6, literally). So after the loss of the temple Jewish Christians (like other contemporary Jews) in principle put ethical demands above ritual demands and here applied the same biblical passage as other Jews. If before the Jewish war (in the Judaizing counter-mission to Paul) they had still vainly sought to integrate the Gentile-Christian communities ritually into Judaism, after AD 70 a transformed Jewish Christianity could make a new attempt to establish its traditions in Gentile Christianity, this time not through ritual demands but through the reinterpreted Jewish ethic of the Jesus tradition. The Gospel of Matthew, which is silent about circumcision and food regulations, is the documentation of this attempt. This attempt had a resounding success. The Gospel of Matthew became the most popular gospel. Its ethically purified Jewish Christianity determined the further history of Christianity. It is thanks to it that the Jewish ethic still shapes Christianity.

But how did the Gospel of Matthew deal with the mono-theistic problem that we detect in Mark? Here it is amazingly open. Already in the baptism God proclaims publicly for all present to hear, 'This is my beloved Son in whom I am well pleased' (3.17). On the basis of the walking on the water the disciples recognize Jesus as a divine being (14.33). A few remnants apart, the mystery of the person of Jesus and the failure of the disciples to understand are suppressed. And yet it is clear from the start that Jesus does not deify himself on his own account. He is attested by the spirit, prophesied by the Old Testament scriptures and announced by prophets. He does not owe his dignity to himself. But above all the Gospel of Matthew (like Q) introduces his appearance with the temptation. And in the temptation on the mountain Jesus shows himself to be an exemplary monotheist. In renouncing the rule of the world offered him by Satan, he underlies his 'humility': he, who is destined to be ruler of the world, goes his way to the cross. Satan's temptation, 'If you are the Son of God, command that these stones be made bread . . .' (4.3; cf. 4.6), finds its echo in the mockery of those who say, 'If you are the Son of God, help yourself and come down from the cross' (27.40). He could have twelve legions of angels at his disposal to defend himself from his enemies (26.53). But he voluntarily renounces his dignity. It is an expression of his ethic that he does not claim divine status for himself. The monotheistic sensitivity of his Jewish tradition can also be traced in Matthew. But does that also apply to Luke and the Acts of the Apostles?

## Luke–Acts

Luke is the only evangelist to contrast the veneration of Jesus with the deification of human beings: Agrippa I and Paul (with Barnabas) are worshipped as gods. Agrippa accepts this worship and dies (Acts 12.19–23); the Christian missionaries risk their lives rejecting it and are rescued (Acts 14.8–20). Despite this clear attitude to any apotheosis of human beings, Luke does not make the absolute distinction between God and human beings to which Jews were accustomed. He quotes with approval words from the Greek poet Aratus, 'We are all ⌐of his (i.e. God's) nature' (Acts 17.28). For him, Jesus is God's son, because all human beings are children of Adam, who is ⌊descended from God (Luke 3.8). All this suggests that Luke was a Gentile. He could have been one of the godfearing Gentiles whom he mentions as sympathizers with the synagogue. He shows how one of these godfearers, the centurion Cornelius, worships Peter as god and has to be enlightened about his error (Acts 10.25–26). It is not the acceptance of a divine nature for human beings that is offensive to Luke but the cultic worship of them. Therefore he can relate without critical commentary how Paul was regarded as a god because he survived a snake-bite, for here Paul is not being worshipped cultically (Acts 28.6). In Luke the protest against the divinization of human beings is fed not so much by the monotheistic sensitivity of Judaism as by antipathy to particular forms of pagan 'idolatry': he rejects the cultic worship of human beings and rulers by acclamation, adoration and sacrifice. Only one person merits them, Jesus. And for Luke, too, he is more than just a human being.

Who was this former Gentile to whom we owe the two-volume work Luke–Acts and whom we call 'Luke' only by convention? The church tradition identifies him with the physician Luke (Col. 4.14), who is the only one to remain with Paul in his imprisonment in Rome (2 Tim. 4.11). Acts in fact suggests by the use of 'we', which begins when Paul moves over to Europe with his companions (16.10ff.), that it was written by a companion of Paul. This 'we' persists until Paul's arrival in Rome (Acts 28.14ff.). Nowadays the 'we' is sometimes interpreted as an indication of a 'we' source which could derive from a companion of Paul, but it is thought improbable that the whole work was written by a companion of Paul. According to Acts Paul was in Jerusalem twice before the Apostolic Council (Acts 9.23ff.; 11.30), according to Paul himself only once (Gal. 1.18ff.). According to Acts the so-called 'apostolic decree' with impositions on Gentile Christians was decided on in the presence of Paul (Acts 15.20, 29); according to Paul there were no such impositions (Gal. 2.10). According to Acts Paul was not one of the twelve apostles – Acts 14.5, 14 is an exception – but Paul would have attacked anyone who put his apostolate in question. Acts has only vague ideas about his doctrine of justification (Acts 13.38). But only a few understood it. The author of Luke–Acts admires Paul, but he does so from a great distance.

He lived in a different time from Paul. In his preface (Luke 1.1–4) he looks back on the chain of tradition of eye-witnesses and evangelists and puts himself in third place. The destruction of the temple already lies further in the distance. The 'times of the Gentiles' (21.24) began with it. He uses the Gospel of Mark. His gospel is first attested by Marcion (*c.* AD 140) and Acts first by Justin (*c.* AD 150). However, there are the following reasons for dating it between 80 and 100. Although he actively attempted to 'follow all things closely' (1.3) and in so doing also collected sources, he does not know Matthew. Either it did not yet exist or it had not yet been circulated sufficiently. So he could have been writing at around the same time – though this 'at the same time' offers considerable scope.

Perhaps we could date his work rather more precisely: Luke dedicates both his books to a 'most excellent Theophilus' (Luke 1.4; Acts 1.1), who is addressed like a Roman governor (Acts 23.26; 24.2; 26.26). His book also has the Roman upper class in view as readers. Nevertheless, at the beginning he has Mary singing a revolutionary song: God 'casts down the mighty from their thrones and raises up the humble' (Luke 1.52). He criticizes the apotheosis of rulers and has Paul put forward the thesis that 'one must obey God rather than men' (Acts 5.29; 4.19). Here he is alluding to the defence of Socrates before his judges in order to impress the educated (Plato, *Apology* 29d). Such emphasis would be most likely to have found an echo after the fall of Domitian in AD 96, when the Roman aristocracy breathed again because this tyranny had come to an end. Domitian had had himself addressed as God (as *dominus et deus*). He suffered the *damnatio memoriae*. The rejection of the self-apotheosis of rulers and their fall, which Luke depicts in the person of a Jewish client prince (Acts 12), could also have counted on assent from the upper class at that time.

Where did Luke write his two volumes? The last trace of the 'we account' is in Acts 28.16ff., 'And so we came to Rome . . .' The reader is meant to believe that the author is in Rome at the end of the work. Perhaps that is a real clue. The first half of Acts is devoted to Peter, the second to Paul. Both died as martyrs in Rome – because of 'envy' (1 Clem. 5.4). The specific circumstances of their deaths may possibly have been painful to the Roman community. Perhaps that is why Acts breaks off before the death of Paul, although it presupposes it (Acts 20.22ff.). Rome lay far enough away from the places in which Paul had conflicts with his rivals, so that these conflicts could fade into the background in Acts. Moreover in Rome Luke could have been prompted by Josephus' history of the Jews, written in the 90s, to compose a similar work about the Christians. But none of that gives us any certainty about the place of its origin. Be this as it may, Luke wrote in one of the great Mediterranean cities, since that is the world in which he lives.

It is puzzling that Acts contains no reference to the letters of Paul. At most there could be an echo of Rom. 15.25–26 in Acts 19.21, where a similar and geographically unusual route from Ephesus to Jerusalem via Macedonia and Achaea is mentioned. But as this corresponds to the historical facts, memories of it could have been preserved independently of the letters of Paul. Given the historical situation, Paul's letters really should have been known to an admirer of his who was familiar with his mission territory, but there are no clear literary allusions to them in Acts. It is not even clear from Acts that Paul was a great letter writer, who governed and influenced his communities with letters. Luke knew primitive Christian letters: the apostles assembled at the Apostolic Council write a letter to the communities in Syria and Cilicia (Acts 15.23ff.). Priscilla and Aquila send Apollos to Corinth with a letter of commendation (Acts 18.27). Only Paul is described as being exclusively an orator and preacher. Is that done to put him on the same level as the other apostles, who are in fact characterized as 'unlearned and simple people' (Acts 4.13)? Does Luke share the high estimation of the oral word of scripture which we also find in Papias (*CH* III 39,4). If there are rather clearer echoes only of the letter to the Romans, could that be explained by the fact that Luke was writing in Rome, where this letter was certainly accessible? Did the other letters of Paul exist only in the East? But Luke uses sources which come from the East, the logia source and the Gospel of Mark! Or were Paul's letters beginning to be forgotten? If Luke had made the effort, he could have had access to them. If he did know the letters of Paul, we must suppose that with his picture of Paul he was deliberately aiming to correct what Paul himself had said. Be this as it may, in his picture of Paul we observe the same intention as in the Deutero-Pauline letters: it stylizes the historical Paul in a way that makes him more acceptable to the church. In Acts an isolated loner, who provoked much conflict, is embedded in the consensus of the apostles.

Whereas Matthew wrote his gospel to bring the ethics of Jesus near to all peoples, Luke had the ambition as a historian to narrate the decisive phase of world history. He borrows the language of the forms of ancient historiography: in the prologue, when he gives an account of sources and pre-decessors; in the dating, by synchronous events of world politics (Luke 2.1ff.; 3.1ff.); in the 'we' account, which is meant to guarantee to readers that he was an eye-witness; and in the many speeches in which ancient historians used to put their interpretation of events into the mouths of figures in the action. But basically he is less a historian than a good story-teller.

His great achievement is often seen in regarding Jesus, because of the delay of the parousia, no longer as the end of

time but as the 'centre of time' (this is the view taken by
Hans Conzelmann): a time of expectation comes before
him and the time of the church afterwards. He has re-
structured the hidden timetable of the divine salvation history
by a tripartite understanding of time. But Luke shares
primitive Christianity's bipartite understanding of time, which
distinguishes only between expectation and fulfilment. For
him, the time since the appearance of John the Baptist is a
time of fulfilment. However, he divides this fulfilment into
three phases: the prelude of the infancy stories, the activity of
Jesus in the middle, and the mission in the present. He can
cope with the delay of the parousia by giving the present a
positive task which is never completed. But it is equally
important to him that the parousia could break in at any time,
so that people must always be ready to appear before God.
That should prompt them to action. For the beginning of
Acts clearly says that instead of asking about the end of the
world, the disciples are to carry on a mission to the ends of
the earth in the power of the Spirit (1.7–8).

What Luke offers is less the theology of a hidden timetable
of divine salvation history than a historical narrative which
forms the basis for the identity of a religious group existing
in the present. It is important for him that this group does
not just come from Judaism; it is Judaism restored – and it
was only the way in which the Jews excluded themselves which
led to the separation of Christians and Jews. Full of sympathy,
in the infancy narrative he depicts the expectations of pious
Jews, which are fulfilled in Jesus. Here he has quite nation-
alistic hopes for the liberation of Israel proclaimed (1.74).
We ask expectantly how this earthly hope for redemption is
compatible with Roman rule. In 2.1ff. this rule enters the
story of Jesus even before the birth of Jesus through an edict
of the emperor Augustus: all the world pays tax to the Romans.
But an idyllic aura lies over the Christmas story: the angels'
message of peace makes it clear that the new king will not
bring any military victories (2.14). Rather, with the appearance
of Jesus, a time is beginning in which the comprehensive
overcoming of evil is tangibly near: in it Jesus brings salvation
to the poor and sick (4.18ff.). At the beginning of Jesus' activity

Satan flees, and enters into Judas again only at the end (Luke 4.13; 22.3). He has lost his power as a result of this activity.

Luke divides this activity of Jesus geographically into three phases: the activity in Galilee (3.21 – 9.50), the journey from Galilee to Jerusalem which he has expanded into his 'travel account' with large parts of the logia source (9.51 – 19.27), and the last days in Jerusalem (19.28ff.). In the middle of the travel account (and his gospel) he puts a chapter with three parables about the lost – culminating in the parable of the lost, prodigal son (15.11–32). Here he expresses the centre of his theology: God cares for all those who turn to him. All – like the prodigal son – are restored to their original states and given a ring, the symbol of royal investiture. Pious and exemplary people are asked whether, like the older brother, they accept this unmerited goodness of God. This is a 'narrative theology' of the forgiveness of sins – with no recourse to an atoning death of Jesus on the cross. In the parable of the prodigal son only a fatted calf is slaughtered, not an expiatory sacrifice. Here and elsewhere in Luke human beings appear not as those who have to be saved by the complete transformation of their being but as those who have to be *corrected* – as those who have to correct their conduct and its direction. The way in which the notion of expiation retreats into the background – it is echoed only in the traditional eucharistic words (22.19–20) and in the 'testament of Paul' (Acts 20.38) – fits the optimistic picture of human beings in which this Gentile Christian stands close to the Jewish-Christian Matthew.

The other gospels break off with the resurrection of Jesus as if they were to relate the activity of the Risen Christ in heaven in the same way as his activity on earth. For them, after Easter, history holds its breath. Eternity breaks into time. How can one narrate this? Luke does so with naïve means. He divides the Easter experience into three acts which he narrates in succession: resurrection, ascension and Pentecost. That results in a sequence of events which can be narrated and has become the foundation of the Christian festivals. In addition, as a delayed Easter appearance, there is the appearance of Jesus to Paul, which he narrates three times

(Acts 9.1ff.; 22.1ff.; 26.4ff.). Thus by narrative means, i.e. though a sequence of events, he indicates that the time since Jesus has been governed by an invasion of time by eternity. This invasion took place through the Spirit, which was active before Jesus in individual Old Testament and Jewish prophets (Luke 3.22; 4.18ff.), but which since Pentecost has been active in all members of the people of God, in sons and daughters, young and old, slaves both men and women (Acts 2.17–18 = Joel 3.1ff.). He does not make such subtle statements about this spirit as Paul, who sees the spirit as an ethical force of the new life. Rather, for him the spirit is a power that expresses itself in visible miracles and glossolalia. It advances the mission – beyond the limits of cultures and languages. It brings about that universalization of the Jewish faith which is at the centre of Paul's thought and action. But it is also the power of conversion. To this degree it also has ethical consequences. What changes does that make to human life?

Luke makes clear statements about this. Jesus defines his mission twice: 'I have not come to call the righteous, but sinners to repentance' (Luke 5.32); 'For the Son of Man has come to seek and save that which is lost' (19.10). The Lukan Jesus says the same thing to the ordinary toll collector Levi and the senior toll collector Zacchaeus: all, high and low, must repent. Jesus goes in search of all who are lost. That is why three parables about the lost stand at the centre of the Gospel of Luke: the lost sheep, the lost coin and the lost son (Luke 15). Their point is that repentance should not be motivated by fear of the judgment but by the joy in heaven which is greater 'over a single sinner who repents than over ninety-nine just men who need no repentance' (15.7). This joy is to find an echo on earth and lead to other shared joy, that of neighbours, friend and brother. By its picture of the human Jesus who seeks the lost and the outsiders, the Gospel of Luke has become inscribed on the hearts of its readers, probably most of all as a result of the parables of the good Samaritan, the prodigal son, and the Pharisee and the toll collector.

In Luke, too, conversion means a new relationship. That is illustrated by two themes: dealing with power and possessions.

The last statement in Acts is that despite his imprisonment in Rome Paul teaches 'unhindered' (Acts 28.31). The unhindered proclamation of the gospel is the concern of the 'political ethics' in Luke–Acts. It is at the same time both a programme and an estimation of the actual situation. Luke wants to make it clear that Christians are valuable citizens. They are loyal and pay their taxes – unlike rebels such as Judas of Galilee (Acts 5.37). They contribute to the *pax romana*. Therefore officials and soldiers can become Christians. Had people listened to Jesus' preaching, even the Jewish war could have been avoided (Luke 19.41–44). Luke is the only New Testament author who associates positive consequences for politics with Christianity. At the same time he contradicts inwardly radical currents in Christianity which are critical of the state. Even if Christians have the impression that Rome is the seat of Satan – and the temptation story in Luke 4.5–7 can certainly be read in this way – Christianity can develop in the Roman empire. Luke wants to tell his communities that this state, too, is an opportunity for Christians. The Roman empire offers the possibility of practising religion freely. Only bad officials are hindering it. But Luke knows limits to the political loyalty of Christians: where preaching is suppressed, civil disobedience is a duty. The self-apotheosis of political authorities is to be rejected. Thus he advocates a critical loyalty to the state. Christianity is politically a valuable contribution to peace, but Christians cannot go along with everything.

What Luke–Acts says about possessions is not intrinsically homogeneous. One could present Luke as both an evangelist of the poor and an evangelist of the rich. There is no disputing the fact that he thinks it important that Christianity should penetrate lofty circles. That makes the 'pauperistic' traits in his work all the more amazing. Mary's Magnificat formulates a programme, 'He (God) fills the hungry with good things and sends the rich empty away' (Luke 1.53). Jesus carries out this 'programme': in his inaugural discourse he defines his mission (with Isa. 60.1–2) as a message of salvation for the poor (4.18), and in the Sermon on the Plain he develops it with beatitudes for the poor, the hungry and those who weep

(6.20–21). Above all he now formulates demands to the
followers of Jesus: Luke interprets love of enemy as an invitation to lend money generously, even if there is no hope of
getting it back again (6.34, 35). He combines the commandment to love, which is central for him, with the theme of
money and possessions. Luke is convinced that riches are
dangerous. In the Sermon on the Plain the Lukan Jesus hurls
woes against the rich (Luke 6.24–25). Luke illustrates the
dangers of wealth by vivid examples: disputes over inheritances
(Luke 12.13–14), illusory trust in riches (Luke 12.16–21), the
fate of the merciless rich man in the other world in the story
of poor Lazarus (Luke 16.19–31), and the unsuccessful calling
of a rich man, which shows how little hope the rich have of
entering the kingdom of God (Luke 18.18–27).

But above all Luke shows how nevertheless one can deal
constructively with one's riches. He knows three possibilities
here: total renunciation of possessions in radical discipleship,
giving away some possessions, and the communism of property
in the primitive community.

1. The disciples forsake 'everything' (Luke 5.11, 28), travel
   without possessions (9.3; 10.4) and are not to be worried
   about anything (12.22ff.). But their radical poverty is
   restricted by the Lukan Jesus himself to the subsequent
   period (Luke 22.35–36). Jesus' disciples are not to go
   through the land and be a burden on settled sympathizers. Luke argues energetically that leaders of communities should, rather, earn their own living – and
   even give away to others what they have earned with
   the work of their hands (Acts 20.32–35). Nevertheless,
   for him radical renunciation of possessions remains a
   possibility of Christian life.

2. Other followers of Jesus give away possessions to a
   moderate degree. Some women support Jesus out of
   their possessions (8.1–3). The chief toll collector
   Zacchaeus gives away half his possessions (Luke
   19.1–10). The parable of the unjust steward is meant
   to motivate people to write off debts and do good
   (Luke 16.1ff.). In Acts Barnabas is a positive example

of such generous giving: he gives the proceeds of the sale of a field to the Jerusalem community (Acts 4.36–37), whereas Ananias and Sapphira are a negative example: they pretend to renounce some of their property, but are not really prepared to give it up (Acts 5.1ff.).

3. Finally, in Acts Luke sketches out a third possible way of dealing with possessions. Granted, initially the theme of riches and poverty seems to fade into the background in Acts. The details are missing but not the matter itself. For here Luke formulates his ideal picture: that of the first Christians sharing their possessions. There must not be any poor people in the Christian community. Rather, all possessions must be common to all. For him this is both the fulfilment of an Old Testament promise in Deut. 15.4 and the ideal widespread in pagan antiquity that friends have everything in common.

The ethics of possession in Luke–Acts has been interpreted in different ways. Does Luke require only those in office to renounce their possessions, while others need engage only in charitable activity? Is he writing for a situation in which many people had lost their possessions as a result of persecution and is now pleading for people to share what they have? Is he formulating an appeal to the rich for donations with an exaggerated ethical rhetoric? None of this fits his ethics of possession. Luke wants to put not the rich, but everyone, under an obligation to support one another. He knows that the ideal of sharing possessions cannot be practised without difficulty. His last statement on the topic is probably his own recommendation. Paul in his farewell speech presents himself as a positive example in saying that he works with his own hands to earn his living – and to have the means of supporting others. For it is more blessed to give than to receive (Acts 20.32–35). Here he is transferring an ancient maxim of benefactors, applied to kings and rich people who give of their superfluity, to ordinary people who only have their labour with which to help others.

## Writing the gospels and directing the community

The origin of the synoptic gospels is the central event in the history of primitive Christian literature. Just as the first basic form of primitive Christianity, the letter, was produced by the Judaistic crisis, so the second basic form, the gospel, was produced by the crisis of the Jewish war and its consequences. All three gospels show connections with the Jewish war. If we ask why the evangelists wrote, in my view we find in them the same motivation as that of Paul in writing his letters. In critical phases he wanted to influence his communities to think like him and to guide them. That challenged him as a writer. The same motivation to produce literature is also at work among the evangelists. They too wanted to guide communities in and after crises. They do not do so by giving direct instructions in letters, but in an indirect way by telling a story about Jesus. They activate the supreme authority in primitive Christianity for the task of guiding the community. If we ask what are the tasks of a leader of the community, we can identify five of them:

1. The leader of the community must express the consensus in the community. He can influence it only if he is rooted in it. The three synoptic gospels gather together traditions and sources about Jesus and from them form a picture of Jesus on which there can be a consensus.

2. The leader of the community must communicate to the community a picture of its environment, so that he can also lead it through crises and conflicts with the environment. All three gospels provide stimuli as to how Christians are to behave in the crisis after the Jewish war.

3. The leader of the community must define Christian identity as distinct from the mother religion of the first Christians. He must answer the question: Why have we separated from the Jews and how far do we nevertheless still belong to them? All three synoptic

gospels are concerned with the relationship between the community and the environment, both with the Roman empire and with Judaism.

4. The leader of the community must resolve tensions in his own community and make it possible for different groups to live together within it. That is always a balancing act. On the one hand he must put forward the shared norms – and possibly see that members who contravene them are excluded. But he must also behave flexibly, so that they are not divided unnecessarily. Here too one can demonstrate that all the gospels seek to resolve internal tensions.

5. The leader of the community must create a structure of authority within the community which is independent of persons and generations. This includes the formulation of criteria of legitimate authority that can be accepted by as many people as possible. This task, too, has left traces in the gospels. Ultimately Jesus is the only legitimate authority in them.

If we look at the three synoptic gospels in the light of these five tasks, we can note that they perform the function of literature which guides the community. To show this, I shall once again go briefly through each of the three gospels.

*(a) The Gospel of Mark*

1. *Formation of consensus.* Mark sets out to create a picture of Jesus on which there can be a consensus by combining two traditions about Jesus: the miracle stories and the passion story. In the miracle stories Jesus overcomes distress and suffering. By contrast, the passion story shows him as a helpless figure who is himself exposed to suffering. Mark combines the two traditions and thus unites two pictures of Jesus. The motifs of secrecy serve to indicate to the reader that he has understood Jesus completely only if he has read the gospel through to the end. It is not

enough simply to take note of the miracle stories. The cross is also part of the gospel.

2. *Orientation on the environment.* The Gospel of Mark sketches a dark picture of the environment. It is an anti-gospel to the gospels of the Flavians after the Jewish war. Jesus, not the Flavians, has saved the world. The community is in opposition to the world and must prepare for conflicts. The Gospel of Mark gives it help when it says that Christians need not needlessly make their identity known in public. Jesus, too, initially wanted to remain secret and unknown. But if God leads the Christians who follow Jesus into conflicts, they are self-confidently to stand by their identity.

3. *Definition of identity.* Mark formulates the identity of Christians in connection with Judaism, yet dissociating them from it. There is no dissent over basic ethical questions (12.38–44), only over ritual questions. The temple (the ritual centre of the Jewish religion) has been destroyed. The old ritual commandments – relating to the sabbath and cleanness – are criticized in Mark. In their place Mark introduces two new Christian rites, baptism and eucharist. The Gospel dissociates itself ritually from Judaism.

4. *Internal tensions.* In the Gospel of Mark we detect internal tensions between itinerant charismatics and local communities. Therefore the evangelist reinterprets discipleship. It consists not only in following Jesus in the literal sense but also in sharing meals (2.15), readiness to suffer (8.34) and care for others (15.41). Family values are reactivated in the face of the non-family ethic of the itinerant charismatics: duties towards parents (7.8–13), wives (10.2–12) and children (10.13–16).

5. *Structures of authority.* The Gospel of Mark bears witness to the process in which local communities detach themselves from the authorities of the first generation, the itinerant charismatics. Readiness for service and martyrdom is a legitimation for authority. Whoever wants to be first must be ready to be last. The

conversation with the sons of Zebedee shows that (10.35–45). The task of the community leader also includes the care of children (who have no parents) (Mark 9.33–37).

## *(b) The Gospel of Matthew*

1. *Formation of consensus.* Whereas the Gospel of Mark combines the miracle and the passion tradition, in Matthew we find a synthesis of Jewish-Christian and Gentile-Christian traditions. Strictly Jewish-Christian material from the Matthaean special material is combined with the Gentile-Christian Gospel of Mark. The basis of this synthesis is the kind of moderate Jewish Christianity that we find in the logia source.

2. *Orientation on the environment.* Matthew proclaims the world rule of a Jewish king and in so doing transforms hopes of a world ruler who, coming from the East, will replace the rule of the Romans. Here he combines Jewish messianic expectations with pagan hopes as embodied by the magicians from the East (Matt. 2.1ff.). He radically redefines messiahship. A militant messiah is replaced by a peaceable king who seeks to rule the world only by his commandments.

3. *Definition of identity.* Matthew formulates an ethical demarcation rather than the ritual demarcation of Judaism. Jews are to practise a 'better righteousness' than Pharisees and scribes (5.20). Matthew therefore emphasizes that Christians have much in common with Jews: the Torah (5.17), the scribes (23.1ff.), the messianic hope. The loss of the temple affects Jews and Christians in the same way. It is met with an activation of the ethical side of Judaism (with Hos. 6.6).

4. *Internal tensions.* Matthew works to resolve tensions between Jewish Christians and Gentile Christians. To do so it outlines a picture of the community as a mixed body in which groups of different origins live together. For this reason Matthew works out the ethic of mutual

forgiveness (6.14): even strong tensions in the community can be coped with by practising it.

5. *Structures of authority.* The Matthaean community is an egalitarian community. 'You have only one teacher, Christ' (23.10). His teaching is formulated in Matthew as if it applied until the end of the world. With this emphasis on the sole authority of Jesus Matthew fundamentally emphasizes the authority of his gospel. With it he influences the communities – passing over the structures of authority that existed in his time.

### (c) Luke–Acts

1. *Formation of consensus.* More than any other evangelist, Luke combines the authority of Jesus with the authority of the apostles by devoting one work to each. Within Acts he creates an equilibrium between the dominance of Peter in the first part (to Acts 15) and the dominance of Paul in the second. The oppositions between the different currents in primitive Christianity are harmonized: his ideal is the primitive community, which was of one heart and one soul.

2. *Orientation on the environment.* Luke sketches a differentiated picture of the environment, in which any painting in black and white is avoided. In it there are good and bad officials, sympathetic and hostile Pharisees, a hardened and a remorseful 'thief' on the cross. This environment offers the opportunity to preach the gospel unhindered. But if need be this opportunity must be defended by civil disobedience. Luke emphasizes that more clearly than any author in the New Testament (with the exception of the Apocalypse of John).

3. *Definition of identity.* In Luke–Acts Luke sketches out the picture of a gradual separation of Jews and Christians. At the beginning the promise of salvation is also extended to Gentiles – with the result that Israel gains (Luke 2.31). Jesus turns only to Israel, but brings about

a split between people and leaders within it. After Easter
the Holy Spirit renews the assembly of Israel successfully,
as is shown by the mass conversions in Acts. Only the
Gentile mission leads to the final repudiation of the
message by Jews. At the end there is a little ray of hope
if we translate the conclusion of Acts 28.27 literally as
future: 'and I will heal them'. At all events the ritual
demarcation in Mark and the ethical demarcation in
Matthew are supplemented with a historical demarcation. Luke relates how the separation came about –
and thus shows that it is unnecessary and need not exist
for all time.

4. *Internal tensions.* Luke–Acts is marked by tensions
   between poor and rich. Luke wants to overcome these
   tensions not only by a vertical balance through the
   giving of the rich but also by a horizontal balance
   between all. John the Baptist already tells people in his
   speech that even ordinary people must share their food
   (Luke 3.10–14), and Paul wants to persuade those who
   work to support one another (Acts 20.32–35).

5. *Structures of authority.* Luke opposes financial support
   for itinerant charismatics and local officials, but also
   the beneficence of the powerful and rich (Luke 2.25).
   For him authority is bestowed by legitimate succession.
   By the activity of the twelve apostles and the thirteenth
   witness, Paul, legitimacy is given to the Samaritan
   Christians (Acts 8.14ff.) and the disciples of John in
   Ephesus (Acts 19.1–7).

If the evangelists wanted to guide the communities by their
writings, they were seeking to fill the gap in authority which
the departure of the first generation had left behind. Here
they wanted to reinforce the authority of Jesus. Any other
authority paled beside that. If we ask in what circles the
evangelists must be sought, we are most likely to find them
among the Christian 'wise men' (Matt. 23.34), 'scribes' (Matt.
13.52) and 'teachers' (Acts 13.1; 1 Cor. 12.29; Eph. 4.11; James
3.1; Did. 13.2) who are mentioned now and then in the
sources. There must have been some intellectuals in primitive

Christianity who, like intellectuals of all times, dreamed of exercising influence through writings – even going beyond the institutionalized authorities. There were also such intellectuals in the Pauline school. Here, however, quite a different course was taken. For the New Testament pseud-epigraphy which came into being at the same time as the gospels, it is not Jesus but the apostle Paul who is the authority towering above everyone else. His letters, authentic and inauthentic, filled the vacuum in authority created by the death of the first generation. By contrast, Paul appears in Luke–Acts only as a model for conversion, as a missionary and miracle-worker, but nowhere as a letter-writer. However, Paul achieved his greatest influence through letters. The pseudepigraphy of primitive Christianity above all bears witness to this.

# CHAPTER 7

# Pseudepigraphical Letters: The Continuation of the Literature of the First Generation

Primitive Christian pseudepigraphy, i.e. letters written under a false name, experienced a heyday at the same time as the gospels. Of twenty-one letters in the New Testament, ten are probably inauthentic: of the Pauline letters, 2 Thessalonians, Colossians, Ephesians and three Pastoral letters (1 and 2 Timothy, Titus); of the Catholic letters 1 and 2 Peter, Jude and James. In addition there is Hebrews which, while it may not claim to come from Paul, wants to suggest to the reader that it does. We are not certain in every case: even critical exegetes believe that Colossians and 2 Thessalonians may be authentic, but conservative exegetes also increasingly believe that they are not. Pseudepigraphy is probable when the historical situation presupposed in the letters, their theology, language and style, indicate a different time from that of the first generation of primitive Christianity.

The discovery of pseudepigraphy in the New Testament made it possible to distinguish between the authentic Paul and the primitive Christian picture of Paul. Up to that point Paul had been read through the filter of letters wrongly attributed to him. When the Pastoral letters exclude women from functions of leadership in the community, we now know that this has nothing to do with Paul. And if they oblige women to marry and have children, today we are certain that this is not what the authentic Paul wanted.

We call inauthentic letters forgeries if they deliberately set out to mislead readers about their true authorship. When in what follows I speak of 'pseudepigraphical letters', or in the Pauline sphere of 'Deutero-Pauline letters', I am deliberately avoiding any moral evaluation. But that must not disguise the fact that even in antiquity 'forgeries' were thought to be reprehensible. At that time, too, there was a concept of intellectual property. When at the end of the second century it emerged that a presbyter had forged the Acts of Paul and Thecla 'out of love of Paul' he had to resign his office (Tertullian, *de baptismo* 17). That makes it even more urgent to ask: how could it come about that Christians with such a high ethic of truth wrote so many inauthentic letters? That is a real challenge for historical understanding.

## The origin of the pseudepigraphy of primitive Christianity

The conditions for pseudepigraphic writings at that time were more favourable than they are today. There was little chance of their being detected on their production. In the school of grammar people practised imitating texts in order to get as close to the original as possible. Primitive Christian authors with some education had had practice in slipping into the role of someone else and writing in his name. However, that only explains how writers were 'technically' in a position to write inauthentic letters, and not why they did so.

Nor is it much of an explanation to say that primitive Christianity stood in the tradition of Jewish pseudepigraphy. Most works of Hellenistic Judaism were published under false names. The exceptions are quickly listed: they include Jesus Sirach, Flavius Josephus and Philo of Alexandria. Against the background of the Jewish writing of the time it is more surprising that there are so many authentic letters in the New Testament than that it contains so many inauthentic ones. But there are important differences from Jewish pseudepigraphy: Jewish writings chose as pseudonymous authors figures from prehistory (like Enoch, Abraham and Moses), whose authority was already given by the Old Testament. Often the choice of such pseudonyms was motivated by a desire in apocalyptic writings to depict the past course of history as fulfilled prophecy, in order to give credibility to prophecies which were still open. This motive is absent from the New Testament. Here names of contemporary figures who were still known to those to whom the letters were addressed served as pseudonyms. In the only apocalypse of the New Testament the author does not hide behind a figure of prehistory. He gives his name, John, and he makes no secret of the fact that he is a contemporary of those whom he is addressing. Moreover, primitive Christian pseudepigraphy was circulated above all in the form of letters. Now letters and collections of letters were widespread as a form of publication in the pagan sphere. Here, for example, there was a collection of letters of Plato, which also included inauthentic letters. So the Jewish tradition of pseudepigraphical letters cannot be made responsible for the pseudonymous letters.

We get closer to the historical state of affairs by noting that oral traditions about Paul (and other apostles) circulated in primitive Christianity. 2 Thessalonians 2.5 recalls an oral tradition of Paul's about a 'man of lawlessness' who 'even sits in the temple of God and claims to be God'. That is why the letter has been written. For only here does 2 Thessalonians clearly go beyond 1 Thessalonians. The Colossians hymn (Col. 1.15–20), or those statements in the Pastoral letters emphasized by the formula 'The saying is sure' (1 Tim. 1.15; 3.1; 4.9; 2 Tim. 2.11; Titus 3.8), could be further Pauline traditions. Disciples of Paul gathered such oral traditions and wrote them down in letter form. They were convinced that they were handing on sayings of Paul. Here we should remember that primitive Christianity was a society of oral communication. Oral traditions were varied, changed and invented depending on the situation. They move from author to author. The awareness of intellectual authorship is weaker than is the case with written tradition.

But the disciples of Paul could also claim Pauline author-ship for what they added in writing. In general the maxim 'What his pupils have published may be regarded as the work of the teacher' (Tertullian, *Adversus Marcionem* IV 5, 4) holds in antiquity. The Pythagoreans thought it right 'to attribute their teachings to Pythagoras and to give them his name and to get no praise of their own for this' (Iamblichus, *De vita Pythagorica* 198). But there was an even closer bond between Paul and his fellow-workers than between a philosopher and his pupils: his fellow-workers were already his representatives in his lifetime. They appeared in the Pauline communities as his messengers and brought his words. In my view the key to the origin of primitive Christian pseudepigraphy lies in this awareness of being representatives. Paul himself encouraged it, as is shown by his commendation of Timothy: 'Therefore I send to you Timothy, my beloved and faithful child in the Lord, to remind you of my ways in Christ, as I teach them everywhere in every church' (1 Cor. 4.17). If Timothy could appear as Paul's spokesman even in Paul's lifetime, why should he not continue this role after Paul's death? That applies to all Paul's fellow-workers. They knew very many more state-ments by Paul than those he left behind in letters. Why should they not publish them under his name?

Paul's fellow-workers might indeed rightly understand themselves as Paul's co-authors. For through their reports from the communities, their reactions and their suggestions for a reply, they were in fact co-authors of his letters. That is why (except in Romans and Galatians) Paul mentions them as co-authors in the introduction to a letter. Certainly they hardly formulated his letters. Timothy, who is mentioned as co-author in Phil. 1.1, certainly did not write of himself, 'I have no one like him, who will be genuinely anxious for your welfare' (2.20). After Paul's death, however, such fellow-workers could have been aware that if they had helped to develop Paul's theology and were regarded by him as co-authors of his letters, they also continued to be his spokesmen. We must not insinuate that they had any intention of forgery to explain why they wrote letters in Paul's name. They thought that they were his authentic voice! So it is certainly no coincidence that the first two pseudepigraphical letters of Paul mention fellow-workers alongside Paul at the head of the letter: Timothy in Col. 1.1, Silvanus and Timothy in 2 Thess. 1.1. Later only Paul appears as author, as in Ephesians and the Pastoral letters. In them Paul has already become the sole authority.

Here, however, among the pseudepigraphical letters we can establish differences in the inter-textual references to the authentic letters of Paul.

- 2 Thessalonians is based on a single letter, 1 Thess-alonians. It could go back to oral traditions of Paul which Paul had left on visits to Thesssaloniki.

- Unlike 2 Thessalonians, Colossians and Philemon do not interpret a single letter but develop the whole of Pauline theology in a speculative way. They have echoes of all the authentic letters of Paul and must have been written by fellow-workers. In both letters Paul is in prison, and thus in the eyes of their authors is dependent on others to act for him.

- The Pastoral letters imitate the collection of Paul's letters. For they were created from the start as a corpus of three letters. They understand themselves to draw on an objective 'deposit' of faith which had been entrusted to Paul to look after. So they have a good conscience in using this 'deposit' independently of him. Their thoughts take quite a different direction from Colossians and Ephesians. We find a matter-of-fact, almost anti-speculative Christianity orientated on practice. Particularly in 2 Timothy we find references to specific situations. The suggestion of authenticity is developed in detail: 'Paul' asks for his cloak and books to be brought from Troas (2 Tim. 4.13). Here we are at the start of deliberate falsification, unless it is assumed that in 2 Tim. 4.9–17 the author has used a fragment from an authentic letter of Paul or historical traditions about him.

- All the letters mentioned so far were published under the name of Paul. In addition the pseudepigraphical

Catholic letters appeared under the name of other apostles and two brothers of the Lord. In them the letter form is governed by the model of Paul's letters. But in content, too, they seek to be a counterbalance to the Pauline letters. The relationship to the authors Peter, James and Jude is formal. It is impossible to recognize a school tradition going back to these figures, even if it is often conjectured in the case of James. In the case of 2 Peter we can perhaps reckon with an 'open pseudepigraphy', i.e. a fictitious reference to Peter which those addressed can immediately see through (see below).

• Finally, mention should be made of the two anonymous letters Hebrews and 1 John, which suggest that they have been composed by Paul or by the author of the Gospel of John respectively, without saying so directly. The letter form is maintained only superficially. Both begin with poetic tones – with the fragment of a hymn in Heb. 1.3, with echoes of the Logos hymn of John 1.1ff. in 1 John 1.1–3. As formally independent letters, in content, too, they advocate a very independent theology.

The explanation of primitive Christian pseudepigraphy sketched out here can dispense with the traditional assumption that the authors understood themselves to be instruments of the Holy Spirit. They themselves are said to have felt this as authors of their writings and it is supposed to have enabled them to attribute their writings to other apostles with a good conscience. This explanation is unconvincing, since particularly the prophetic writings which understood themselves to be 'inspired' mention their real authors: the Revelation of John and the Shepherd of Hermas. Primitive Christian pseudepigraphy is not explained by a sense of inspiration but by the claim of Paul's fellow-workers to be representing him. That enabled them to write inauthentic letters without falsification and disseminate them as letters of Paul. The gap in authority after the departure of the first generation is a further explanation why the production of inauthentic letters rose in the period between AD 70 and AD 130. That was the time when it was practised. Finally, the existence of a living Pauline school explains why most of the pseudepigraphical letters were attributed to Paul. Here a claim by Paul's fellow-workers to be representing him could arise 'naturally'. In what follows I cannot introduce each of these letters appropriately, but will content myself with showing that all the pseudepigraphical letters in the New Testament develop and correct the authentic letters of Paul. That was often the reason why they were written. But they do not go into this reason. They always also indicate a theological world of their own.

## The Deutero-Pauline letters

### (a) 2 Thessalonians

2 Thessalonians imitates 1 Thessalonians in form, in order to say the opposite in content. 1 Thessalonians has the expectation of an imminent end; 2 Thessalonians warns against it. In it 'Paul' recalls that during his stay he taught that before the end a 'man of lawlessness' had to come 'who opposes and exalts himself against every so-called god or object of worship, so that he takes his seat in the temple of God, proclaiming himself to be God' (2.4). Before he appears, 'he who now restrains it' (2.7) must be removed. Here in my view we have traces of experiences with Gaius Caligula, who in AD 39/40 wanted to erect his statue in the Jerusalem temple. After his murder it was expected that another emperor would carry out his plan, which was thought only to have been postponed. Something was delaying this hybrid plan. Ideas of this kind could go back to the 40s or 50s. Paul certainly never put them forward during his first stay in Thessaloniki. But he visited the community again later (2 Cor. 2.13; Acts 20.1ff.). And he will have been asked there why the imminent end that he had announced in 1 Thessalonians had not come about. At that time Paul could have corrected his first letter orally – by teaching about what was delaying the end. Later, someone then felt justified in working out Paul's correction of himself as 2 Thessalonians and publishing it. So 2 Thess. 2.5 recalls

what Paul said when he was in Thesssaloniki. And it openly
warns against reading the expectation of an imminent end
out of 1 Thessalonians: 'Do not be quickly shaken in mind
or excited, either by spirit or by word, or by letter purporting
to be from us, to the effect that the day of the Lord has
come' (2.2). Does 2 Thessalonians here want to declare that
the rival 1 Thessalonians is inauthentic? Hardly! The quotation imitates only the sense of 1 Thessalonians, not the
actual words. Moreover the community is to hold on to
the traditions of Paul – both in oral and in written form.
1 Thessalonians is explicitly confirmed, but its interpretation
is to be corrected. The author is saying: if there is a letter
with such an expectation of an imminent end, this cannot
come from Paul. But if it does come from Paul, it cannot
contain an expectation of an imminent end of this kind.
All this was no theoretical problem. In the paraenetical section
2 Thessalonians criticizes members of the community who
want to stop working. Have some of them neglected their
daily duties, appealing to the imminent end? But in that
case how could they have persuaded the others to feed them?
Is it more probable that the expectation of an imminent end
led to an unusual readiness to support one another? The
author explicitly praises the community: 'the love of every
one of you for one another is increasing' (1.3). Before he
confirms his warning against people who are work-shy, he
confirms the eschatological expectation: they are to wait for
Christ unswervingly (3.5). Their readiness to give social
support in view of the imminent end has been exploited. But
the author did not want to admonish them to practise less
mutual love. He does not criticize the excessive zeal of the
givers but the reluctance of the recipients to work – with a
slogan which has become a proverb: 'If anyone *will* not work,
let him not eat' (3.10). So the expectation of an imminent
end probably did not so much motivate some idlers to stop
working as motivate the community to support some people
who were living as parasites. The Didache also warns against
such an exploitation of the readiness of communities to
provide support (Did. 11–12).

## (b) Colossians

Colossians and Philemon belong together. They have many names in common: Timothy, Archippus, Onesimus, Epaphras (the fellow-prisoner in Philemon is the founder of a community in Colossians), and also Jesus (Justus), Mark, Aristarchus, Demas and Luke. If the information about them were inaccurate, given the close chronological proximity of Colossians to Paul it could have very quickly been denied and thus also have compromised Colossians. We may assume that this circle of fellow-workers really existed and that the personal information about it in Colossians is historically accurate. In Colossians this group is fighting against a 'philosophy' (2.8) in which the world has undergone a religious transfiguration. Its central demand was that people should obey the elements of the world and be subject to them. It is less clear what philosophy this was – possibly it was a variant of Neo-Pythagoreanism. At all events it was one of those re-sacralizing philosophies which were typical of the period of the first centuries AD. All philosophical currents of that time were seized with a longing for the divine. All competed with religion. Against this self-sacralizing philosophy Colossians says that it is not the world interpreted in numinous terms but only a man who has been crucified and has risen again who has the power to impose religious obligations. Only in him is there a reconciliation of what is in conflict in the world (1.20). Only he overcomes its destructive power (2.15). Colossians takes its decisive statements from a hymn which it first quotes in 1.15–20 and then expounds in 2.8–23 in terms of the acute problem. This hymn was regarded as an authentic tradition of Paul. It put Christ as reconciler at the centre. A religious tie to him means freedom from all the powers of the world. But the solemnity of this religious independence is only just beginning to have an effect on social life. Certainly, according to Colossians, too, among Christians there are no Greeks and Jews, aliens, Scythians, slave and free (3.11). The divisive power of social distinctions has been overcome. But Colossians seems all the more to be insisting (in its so-called 'household table') that women, children and slaves should be submissive. Here,

however, the limitations of men, fathers and masters, are also
pointed out (Col. 3.18 – 4.1). Given the (relatively detailed)
admonitions addressed to slaves, one has the impression that
Colossians is going back somewhat on the letter to Philemon.
Its admonition to slaves is, 'For the wrongdoer will be paid
back for the wrong he has done, and there is no partiality'
(3.25). Had the letter to Philemon aroused great expectations
among slaves, which led them to suppose that the community
would always support them in their everyday conflicts with
their masters?

### (c) Ephesians

Ephesians is modelled on Colossians. In the Pauline circle in
which Colossians was written, a second edition of that letter
was needed (even before AD 100) in which Paul's theology
was developed further. Unlike Colossians, this new version
contains no polemic; on the contrary, over and above
Colossians it emphasizes that Paul's message reconciles Jewish
and Gentile Christians and overcomes the hatred between
Jews and Gentiles (Eph. 2.11–22). Paul, who was a burden on
social peace between Christians and Jews all his life, is here
promoted to the role of the great apostle of peace. This
certainty may have corresponded to a longing in Paul, but it
contradicted reality. His disciples had sensed that Paul could
only become a teacher of the church as a peace-making
apostle. They also toned down his unwieldy teaching
elsewhere. Thus for Paul there was an unbridgeable tension
between marriage ties and religious ties. Married couples are
split between their partners and the Lord (1 Cor. 7.32ff.).
Ephesians makes this competition into a harmonious model
relationship (by developing the household tables in Colossians
further): marriage is an image of the relationship of Christ to
his church. It is stamped by a patriarchalism mitigated by love,
in which the husband takes over the role of the Christ who
surrenders himself (and not that of the ruler). But here too
he remains superior, as Christ is superior to the church. It is
important for Ephesians that anyone can lead a holy life; the
union of the sexes belongs in this holy life as a depiction of

the mystery of the church (Eph. 5.22–33). Rarely in the New Testament is sexuality as highly valued as it is here. An aura of holiness lies over it. Here and elsewhere in Ephesians the longing for great harmony and unity breaks through. Christ is the one who sums up everything in himself and brings it to unity. The church is the forerunner of this unity of humankind. And the union of the sexes is the image of this unity.

It is possible that Ephesians was conceived from the start for a collection of Paul's letters. If we put the letters of Paul in the sequence that is usually preferred, it is striking that they are arranged in order of length, and that this principle begins again twice. In each case the figures below give the number of consonants in the Greek text.

| Original collection | | First appendix | | Second appendix | |
|---|---|---|---|---|---|
| Romans | 34,410 | *Ephesians* | 12,012 | *1 Timothy* | 8,869 |
| 1 Corinthians | 32,767 | Philippians | 8,009 | *2 Timothy* | 6,538 |
| 2 Corinthians | 22,280 | *Colossians* | 7,897 | *Titus* | 3,733 |
| Galatians | 11,091 | 1 Thessalonians | 7,423 | | |
| | | *2 Thessalonians* | 4,055 | | |
| | | Philemon | 1,575 | | |

The new start to the ordering principle indicates an appendix to an already existing collection. In a second 'edition' a second group of letters was added to an original collection of authentic letters (Romans, 1 and 2 Corinthians and Galatians), in which authentic and inauthentic letters alternated: *Ephesians*, Philippians, *Colossians*, 1 Thessalonians, *2 Thessalonians*, Philemon (the inauthentic letters are indicated in italics). From the start Ephesians was conceived of as the introductory letter to this appendix. That explains why it gives no address in the introduction. It addresses just the 'saints there'. The 'in Ephesus' added in the translations is a secondary addition to the text. In his collection of the letters of Paul the author read as a title (even before the introduction to the letter) 'To the Romans', 'To the Corinthians', 'To the Galatians'. He continued by writing 'To the Ephesians', but forgot that such details of the address did not belong to the original letters but only to the collection as a whole. Because he wanted from the start to continue the collection of the letters of Paul, he could content himself with a reference to this title and address the letter to 'the saints there' (namely the Christians in Ephesus, 1.1). We also have good reasons for conjecturing where the first appendix to the letters of Paul was created, in Ephesus. For it was there that the four letters of the original collection were best known: Romans perhaps through a copy sent to Ephesus, 1 and 2 Corinthians and Galatians because they were written wholly or in part in Ephesus. The introductory letter of the appendix addressed to Ephesus therefore probably indicates the place where the letters of Paul were first supplemented.

### (d) The Pastoral letters

The ordering principle begins once again with the Pastoral letters: again in a third edition of an already existing collection of Paul's letters a supplement was added. Again we find references to connections with Ephesus: the fictitious situation in 2 Timothy is that Paul has left Timothy behind in Ephesus and is now teaching him how to lead the community. Perhaps this is an indication that Timothy and Titus (the supposed recipients of the Pastorals) put forward the teachings contained in them. In that case we would have here not so much Pauline traditions as Timothy and Titus traditions. In terms of content these are pragmatic instructions about leading the community. The notions of the community are not very Pauline. The image of the body of Christ in which all members have equal rights is absent. It is replaced by the image of the house presided over by a single *pater familias*: the bishop, who has deacons alongside him and at the same time is embedded in a college of presbyters. Here the Pastorals fuse two constitutions for the community: one deriving from the Pauline sphere with bishops (*episkopoi*) at the head, and another deriving from Jewish Christianity with a presbyterate as the leading organ. At all events, the leadership of the community is institutionalized and restricted. Only men may stand at the head of the community. For women are not to teach (1 Tim. 2.12), and a bishop is to be 'capable of teaching'

(3.2). For Paul every Christian still had a charisma (a gift to contribute to the leadership of the community); in the Pastorals only the bishop has a charisma (2 Tim. 1.6). Paul regarded celibacy as a superior form of life to marriage; by contrast the Pastorals want to oblige women to marry and fight against sexual asceticism – probably because it gives women an independence which seems to them to be suspicious. Paul writes a letter to the master of a slave, and the household tables in Colossians still admonish both slaves and masters in a certain symmetry, but in the Pastorals we find admonitions only to slaves, not to masters: 1 Timothy 6.1–2 fears for the good reputation of Christianity if Christian slaves do not heed their (Christian) masters sufficiently – if they take the letter to Philemon seriously and call for a brotherly relationship between slave and slave-owner. In all these corrections to the authentic Paul it is striking that precisely where the Pastorals directly oppose statements of the authentic letters of the Paul, the author makes his Paul speak in the first person. He knows that on these points he cannot carry conviction by a new interpretation of the Pauline texts but only by an (alleged) retractation from Paul himself. Here are the two most important instances of what Annette Merz has called 'fictitious references to his own text'. They speak for themselves: 'I permit no woman to teach or to have authority over men; she is to keep silent' (1 Tim. 2.12). 'So I would have younger widows marry, bear children, rule their households, and give the enemy no occasion to revile us' (5.14). The fact that the fictitious first person of Paul is inserted here in particular shows that it is an important concern of the Pastorals to keep women from positions of leadership in the community. They are not to teach, but to marry and have children. Without the Pastorals the New Testament would be much more friendly to women.

## The Catholic letters

With the Catholic letters the conditions of the origin of pseudepigraphical writings change. Paul's legacy continued to have influence in a living Pauline school (probably with its centre in Ephesus). But there is no Petrine school behind the letters of Peter and no similar school behind the letter of James. Rather, these pseudonymous names indicate general currents in primitive Christianity: Peter stands for the whole of Christianity; James and Jude stand for Jewish Christianity. And the letters attributed to them are always concerned to correct Paul, or Paulinism after Paul.

*(a) 1 Peter*

1 Peter makes a claim on the whole church for Pauline theology by putting it in the mouth of Peter. But here too Paul is *de facto* corrected. The paraenesis about the state in 1 Peter 2.11–17 puts new emphases by comparison with Rom. 13.1–7: there is no prohibition against resistance. The state is an order created by human beings. It has the task of punishing evil and promoting good. Christians are to collaborate in this as free persons. The emperor is treated like anyone else; the admonitions 'Honour all men,' 'Honour the emperor,' use the same verb and stand on the same level. But how are Christians to be active as free individuals in their society? They are on the one hand elect, priests and kings (2.9). They have broken with meaningless traditions (1.18), indeed they have been redeemed from these traditions – a quite remarkable statement in antiquity, since respecting the tradition of the fathers is one of its basic values. It is understandable that because of such far-reaching deviations from the consensus of the time, Christians are not popular. So on the other hand they are discriminated against. But they have the obligation to endure this discrimination patiently in a world which rejects them, so that 'though speaking against you as wrongdoers, they may see your good deeds . . .' (2.12). The tension between inner superiority over the environment and 'submission' to its discriminations is tremendous – and leads to a differentiated theology of suffering. It is a suffering with Christ, as in the case of Paul. Suffering deliberately accepted by Christians is to serve as a summons to the world around: 'So that, when you are abused, those who revile your good

behaviour in (fellowship with) Christ may be put to shame'
(1 Peter 3.16). Suffering as disciples of Christ is demonstrative
self-stigmatization with which one sets out to disturb and
convert the world around.

### (b) James

Unlike 1 Peter, James does not set out to develop Paul but to
correct him. Paul's conflicts with the Judaizers had left behind
a distorted picture of Jewish Christianity. It is said to put the
unity of the community in question because of ritual commandments, to limit the freedom of the gospel, and to have
an excessive opinion of its authorities: it attaches all too much
importance to its 'pillars' (cf. Gal. 2.1–10). At the end of the
first century none of this applied any longer. For Jewish
Christianity after the loss of the temple, ethics had replaced
rites. It no longer emphasized ritual demands, as in the time
of Paul. James says nothing about them. The Gospel of
Matthew and James are witnesses to this transformed Jewish
Christianity, which concentrated wholly on its ethical
traditions. James shares some traditions with the Gospel of
Matthew. There are echoes of the beatitudes on the poor
from the Sermon on the Mount in James 2.5: 'Has not God
chosen those who are in the world to be rich in faith and
heirs of the kingdom . . . ?' The beatitude on the peacemakers
is echoed in James 3.18: 'And the harvest of righteousness is
sown in peace by those who make peace.' The prohibition of
oaths in the Sermon on the Mount appears in a parallel
tradition in James 5.12. Both the Gospel of Matthew and James
(together with the Didache) are impressive witnesses to a
renaissance of Jewish Christianity after the Jewish war. This
has to defend itself in James. James knows that many deny
that the simple Jewish Christians have a higher (speculative)
wisdom (as in Colossians and Ephesians). So he begins with a
petition for wisdom – but defines it as the strength to lead a
consistent life (James 1.5ff.). This wisdom as a practical way
of life also includes accord between words and deeds (1.22ff.).
The law of freedom requires this accord with itself and is
therefore not, as Paul insinuated, a law of unfreedom but a

law of freedom (1.25). James defends Jewish Christianity in three little treatises:

1.  In the first treatise about personal reputation (2.1–13) he deals with the charge that Jewish Christians like James think too much of their status. Paul had once critically remarked with reference to James and other 'pillars' in Jerusalem that there is no respect of persons before God (Gal. 2.6ff.). James 2.1ff. makes it clear that James regards false respect for senior figures as an offence against the commandment to love. Among Christians there may be no respect of persons.

2.  The second treatise (2.14–26) is about the relationship between faith and works. Paul had given them the impression that Jewish Christians wanted to be justified by 'works'. He had contrasted with this the example of Abraham, who was justified only by his faith. Against this use of the example of Abraham James emphasizes that Abraham was not justified by faith alone but also on the basis of his action. The two must coincide.

3.  The third treatise (3.1–12) is about the power of the tongue. It is immediately continued by remarks about the wisdom from above and from below (3.13–18). Here defence perhaps already goes over to attack. James complains that so many people want to become teachers. But that leads to conflict. It also applies to the speculative wisdom of the Pauline school. He measures any wisdom by its social compatibility. What use is a wisdom which produces only strife and conflict?

Thus James (in the name of James, the brother of the Lord, who was executed in 62) campaigns for a liberal and tolerant Jewish Christianity. James is an apologia for Jewish Christianity against the distorted picture left behind by Paul's conflicts.

*(c) Jude*

In the name of Jude, the brother of the Lord, the letter of Jude attacks false teachers of whom it is said: 'They reject the power of the Lord (*kyriotes*) and blaspheme the supernatural powers' (Jude 8). Criticism of the powers was widespread in the Pauline sphere in particular. In Colossians Jesus triumphs over them (the *kyriotetes*) (Col. 1.16). There is a warning against worshipping angels (2.18). The letter of Jude is outraged by so much impiety. Even the archangel Michael did not dare to blaspheme the devil (Jude 9).

### (d) 2 Peter

Jude was accepted in 2 Peter. 2 Peter too wants to correct Paul. He warns against false interpretation of the letters of Paul. But the example that he cites is not very convincing. It is all too clear that he himself wants to establish a one-sided interpretation of Paul's eschatology. After warning against any expectation of an imminent end, he writes, 'And count the forbearance of our Lord as salvation. So also our beloved brother Paul wrote to you according to the wisdom of all his letters' (2 Peter 3.15–16). Precisely the opposite applies: Paul held firm to the expectation of an imminent end in all his letters. But 2 Peter wants him to be understood quite differently. His problem is the delay of the parousia. How does he cope with it? He points out that: (1) A thousand years are like a day before God. (2) The delay gives an opportunity for repentance. (3) The end will come as unexpectedly as a thief (2 Peter 3.3–10). If nevertheless people mock the failure of the imminent end to materialize, Peter has already prophesied that and refuted it in advance (3.3ff.) In the case of 2 Peter we could have a false attribution of authorship which the contemporary reader would see through – an open pseudepigraphy with no intent to deceive. It is too plain that Peter is on the one hand warning against false teachers after him and on the other acting as if he is contemporaneous with them. These false teachers say that the fathers are dead – yet Peter himself is one of them (2 Peter 3.4).

### Hebrews

Hebrews is the most independent of the post-Pauline letters. Nowhere does it claim Pauline authorship. But when the author says that he wants to meet Timothy and come with him to those to whom the letter has been sent (Heb. 13.23), the name of Paul's closest fellow-worker is meant to form a link with Paul himself. The reader is to make the pseudepigraphical connection which the highly educated author does not want crudely to make himself. The theology of Hebrews is in fact one of the three great theological schemes in the New Testament alongside those of Paul and the Gospel of John. In it Christianity is depicted in cultic categories; in this way an identity problem of the new religion is dealt with. All religions in antiquity had temples, priests and sacrifices, but not the Christians. After the destruction of the temple, that was manifest and final. In this situation Hebrews says that the Christians, too, have a temple: the whole world with heaven and earth. And they also have a high priest, Christ, who as high priest has entered the heavenly sanctuary. They too have sacrifices: the unique sacrifice of Christ which puts an end to all other sacrifices. Christ assumes the role of the high priest who was allowed to enter the holy of holies once a year. Christians will follow him once he has led the way. He is their forerunner. Through him they will also become 'high priests' and acquire the privilege of entering the holy of holies. But life directed towards this destination is not just a matter of entering into the cosmic sanctuary or festival; it involves wandering through the wilderness of life (Heb. 3.7–19) and the dangers of history (11.1ff.) On this journey endurance has to be shown. There is a risk in lagging behind. For there is only one chance of repentance (Heb. 6.4ff.). Cultic sections in which the readers (as at the beginning of Hebrews) already look into heaven, and paraenetic parts in which they are encouraged to persist on laborious ways, alternate. Both agree on one point: there is only *once* an effective sacrifice, when Jesus entered the holy of holies. And conversion happens only *once* in any life. For a long time Hebrews continued to be controversial (above all in the Western church) because of its rejection of a second repentance.

I have been able to discuss the pseudepigrapha only from a limited perspective. They contain many interesting notions

and ideas over and beyond what has been said here. From
the new approaches in their theology I can emphasize here
only a developed 'awareness of revelation' that they have in
common. We often find in them the so-called 'revelation
scheme' – the notion that the mystery of salvation had been
long hidden but now has been made manifest in Christ – as if
there had not previously been a history of revelation in the
Old Testament (cf. the inauthentic conclusion to Romans in
16.25–27; Col. 1.26–27; Eph. 3.4–5, 9; 1 Peter 1.20; 2 Tim.
1.9–10). In the second generation primitive Christianity
became increasingly conscious of depicting something new
that does not involve simply continuing to write out the
tradition. It is based on a revelation which, though in the
midst of time, nevertheless comes directly from God. This
development finds its culmination in the Johannine writings.

# CHAPTER 8

# Johannine Writings: The Link between Gospel and Letter Literature

The two streams of tradition which have been set down in letters and synoptic gospels come together in the writings of the Johannine circles. Here they form a synthesis in both form and content.

In terms of form they combine the gospel and the letter and in so doing serve as a model for the New Testament canon, which consists of two basic forms. The letters derive their authority from the apostles. In the gospels Jesus rises to become the sole authority. The Gospel of John combines both developments: on the one hand in it Jesus is the only 'apostle' (= the one sent by God). And the beloved disciple is his interpreter, who is superior even to the first of the apostles, Peter.

There is also a synthesis in terms of content in the Johannine writings. On the one hand in Paul we found belief in the pre-existent and exalted one with divine status. On the other hand in the synoptic gospels the tradition of the earthly one was permeated by the loftiness of the exalted one without there being any belief in the pre-existence of Jesus in them. In the Gospel of John the two pictures of Jesus are fused. Jesus is pre-existent and belongs to the heavenly world. After his incarnation and before his return to the Father he acts like a god walking over the earth. Doubts in his incarnation are condemned (1 John 4.2). In him the earthly one becomes transparent to the heavenly revealer. Here the Johannine writings present a theology of revelation akin to the scheme of revelation in the post-Pauline letters: in the time before Jesus no one saw God (John 1.18). Only Jesus reveals the 'eternal life which was with the Father' (1 John 1.2). Jesus is the revealer. He proclaims of himself what is proclaimed about him in the Pauline and Johannine letters. Therefore in the Gospel of John the basic problem of primitive Christian religion comes to a head: did Jesus deify himself? This charge is laid against him twice (John 5.18; 10.33).

## The Gospel of John

Where was the Gospel of John composed? Does the fact that the word for 'palm branch' (John 12.13) is an Egyptian word point to Egypt? But the palm plantations in Jericho were owned by Egyptians. The word could have spread round Palestine from there. Or does the Gospel of John come from the territory of King Herod II Agrippa in north-eastern Palestine? For Jews still had political power there at the end of the first century and could threaten Christians, which seems to be presupposed in the Gospel of John. That is not impossible. But the proximity to Ignatius of Antioch also suggests northern Syria: Ignatius, too, calls the eucharistic elements 'flesh and blood' and not 'body and blood' (IgnPhilad. 4.1). He too knows the designations of Jesus as 'door' and 'logos' (IgnPhilad. 9.1; IgnMagn. 8.2). He too speaks of his incarnation in the flesh (IgnEph. 7.2). At all events the prehistory of the Gospel of John leads to Palestine. John 4 shows unusual familiarity with local affairs in Samaria. Here the unknown little place 'Sychar' appears as a Samaritan place. In fact it was the central settlement of the Samaritans in the period between the destruction of Shechem at the end of the second century BC and the foundation of Neapolis in AD 70. There were probably Christians there. For whereas elsewhere in the Gospel of John the world rejects Jesus, in this city it welcomes him with open arms. When Jesus is later accused of being a Samaritan and having a demon (8.48), he rejects the charge of being possessed but not that of being a Samaritan. There must therefore be some connection between

the Gospel of John and the mission to Samaria, though that
does not mean that we can locate the Gospel of John there.
For this mission is indeed connected with a missionary
movement which embraced all Syria (Acts 8.24ff.; 11.19ff.).
However, since Irenaeus the traditional view has sought the
place of the composition of the Gospel of John not in the
East but in Asia Minor. There Passover and Easter were
celebrated according to the Johannine calendar and not that
of the synoptics. There the Montanists (a prophetic movement
in the middle of the second century) appealed to the
Johannine Paraclete. There the Gospel of John was associated
with the Revelation of John. It is there that beyond doubt it
had the greatest influence in the second century. But does
that mean that it was composed there? The location of the
gospel in Ephesus could have been connected with the
(secondary) identification of the evangelist with the author
of the Apocalypse of John. For the latter clearly belongs in
Asia Minor, though it comes from Palestine. As the Gospel of
John must have had a prehistory in the region of Palestine-
Syria, there is still much to be said for the proposal that two
approaches to locating it should be combined: the Johannine
circle could originally have belonged in the East and then
moved to Asia Minor. It brought the gospel into a region
in which the letter form dominated. Therefore it was
supplemented with letters: 1 John presents a treatise aimed
at arriving at a consensus over the theology contained in
the Gospel of John in a new environment. But all that is
controversial.

We can say rather more clearly when the Gospel of John
was written. The identification in John 4.20–21 of the temple
on Gerizim, which has already been destroyed, with Jerusalem
means that in the meantime the Jerusalem temple will have
been destroyed. That also fits the fear of the Jewish aristocracy
that 'the Romans will come and take away the holy places
and the people' (11.48). The end of Jewish autonomy in
Palestine came in AD 70. In 7.49 the Sanhedrin pronounces a
'curse' on the people 'who do not understand the law'. This
could be an allusion to the curse on the heretics which was
included in the synagogue prayer in the 80s. It was not

specifically directed against Christians but against all heretics (just as John 7.49, too, is not specifically directed against Christians). But Christians, too, could not join in pronouncing this 'heretics' blessing' in the synagogue service. It drove them to exclude themselves from the synagogue. If we follow the Gospel of John, in addition this must rather later also have turned into a formal exclusion from the synagogues which is depicted as being partly in the past (9.22; 12.42) and partly in the future (16.2). It cannot be identical with the 'heretics' blessing'. For exclusion is an active procedure against a minority. This brings us to the time between around AD 100 and AD 120 as the time of the composition of the Gospel of John. The earliest extant New Testament papyrus fragment (Papyrus 52) is of John; it used to be dated to around 125, but according to more recent investigations could also be clearly later.

The Gospel of John was certainly not composed all in one piece. It has two conclusions, in 20.30–31 and in 21.24–25, and it contains two farewell discourses of Jesus: one in the form of a dialogue in 13.31 – 14.31 and one in the form of a monologue in 15.1 – 17.26. The conclusion to the first farewell discourse indicates that it was originally continued directly in 18.1: Jesus announces the coming of Judas and says to his disciples, 'Arise, let us be going' (14.31). 18.1 picks this up: 'After these words Jesus went out with his disciples . . .' Thus the Gospel of John was produced in two editions. In the second, not only chapter 21 but also the second farewell discourse was added – as a kind of reinterpretation and deepening of the first farewell discourse. Further parts could also belong to this second edition. There may be dispute over the details of how the Gospel of John grew, but it can hardly be disputed that it had a lengthy origin.

Other gospels must have been known to the writer of the Gospel of John, even if he does not take them over as a source. The basic outline resembles that of the Gospel of Mark: it begins with John the Baptist and ends with the passion narrative. As it is improbable that the same genre was 'invented' twice independently, the evangelist must have known the Gospel of Mark as a whole – not necessarily in writing, but by hearing it read aloud. That too fits Syria, if the Gospel of Mark was composed there.

The Gospel of John is one of the first new interpretations of Christian faith in which one notices a dissatisfaction with traditional Christianity. That becomes clearest in its eschatology. The first Christians expected the kingly rule of God, the parousia, the resurrection and judgment as future events. But a light always shone from these events on the present. The conviction that in their beginnings these things are already being realized now is characteristic of primitive Christian faith from Jesus to the Apocalypse of John. Now the Gospel of John makes these present statements the basis of faith and forces the statements about future to the periphery. The reinterpretation of the parousia in the first farewell discourse is very impressive. At the beginning Jesus announces that he is leaving the disciples to prepare a place for them among the many 'dwellings' with the Father, and then promises his parousia in the traditional sense: then 'I will come again and will take you to myself, that where I am, you may be also' (14.3). But at the end he promises all who love him, 'If a man loves me, he will keep my word, and my Father will love him, and we will come to him and make our home with him' (14.23). Now the dwellings of salvation are no longer in heaven but in human hearts. Now Jesus no longer prepares dwellings with the Father, but his followers are to prepare a dwelling within themselves for the Father and Jesus. The parousia, which previously was identified with Easter, is spoken of in an almost mystical language: 'Yet a little while, and the world will see me no more, but you will see me; because I live, you will live also. In that day you will know that I am in my Father, and you in me, and I in you' (14.19–20). The same is true of eternal life: it is not (just) something in the future. In 17.3 it is defined as knowledge of God: 'And this is eternal life, that they know you the only true God and Jesus Christ whom you have sent.' The resurrection and judgment are not (just) future events. Rather, 'He who hears my word and believes him who sent me, has eternal life; he does not come into judgment, but has passed from death to life' (5.24). And the judgment already takes place now in the human heart, when people accept Jesus or reject him: 'He who believes in me is not judged; he who does not believe in me is judged already' (3.18).

As a result of this shifting of eschatological salvation into human life in the present, Jesus and his message become a timeless confrontation with the eternal God. Christ is the heavenly emissary through whom God becomes accessible. His image is modelled on the notion of the messenger, which was widespread at that time. There are six motifs in the Johannine 'sending christology'.

1. The messenger is sent. The most frequent designation of God in John is 'the Father who has sent me'. The sending of Jesus presupposes his pre-existence. In 3.16–17 it is combined with the traditional notion of Jesus' self-surrender. 'For God so loved the world that he gave his only Son, that all who believe in him should not perish but have eternal life. For God did not send his Son into the world to judge the world, but that the world should be saved through him' (3.16–17).

2. The messenger has to legitimate himself. The Gospel of John calls his legitimation his 'testimony'. Jesus has a better testimony than John the Baptist: his works, God's voice itself and scripture (John 5.31ff.). Basically he legitimates himself through his word (8.13ff.).

3. A messenger must introduce himself. The heavenly emissary does that through his 'I am' sayings: I am the bread of life, the light of the world, etc. (6.35; 8.12; 10.7, 9, 11; 11.25; 14.6; 15.1, 5).

4. A messenger has a task or a 'commandment'. Jesus twice defines this task, once as a commandment to reveal life (12.50) and then as a 'new commandment' to love (13.34).

5. The messenger returns to the one who has sent him. Jesus keeps talking about going to the Father. He says to Mary Magdalene, 'I am going to my Father and your Father, to my God and your God' (20.17).

6. The messenger gives an account of the fulfilment of his task. In the Gospel of John this happens in Jesus' 'high-priestly prayer' even before he returns to the Father (ch. 17). There Jesus says to God, 'I have glorified you on earth and accomplished the work you gave me to do' (17.4).

The special character of this 'messenger' from heaven is that he himself is the essential content of his message. Jesus proclaimed theocentrically the kingdom of God (in the synoptics). Paul proclaimed christocentrically the crucified and risen Christ. In the Gospel of John the proclamation of the earthly Jesus has itself become christocentric. He proclaims himself. And in the encounter with him, salvation and damnation are decided here and now. The life in the present that he discloses cannot be surpassed in all eternity; the salvation that he bestows cannot be denied by the Last Judgment. It is final. It is eschatological salvation in the midst of time.

However, the sending christology is only one side of the christology of the Gospel of John. In it Jesus is subordinate to God as his messenger. But this subordination is balanced by statements according to which Jesus is on the same level as God. Only in the Gospel of John is Jesus called 'God': at the beginning of the prologue (1.18) and at the end, when Thomas addresses him as 'my Lord and my God' (20.28). The divinization of Jesus reaches its climax in the Gospel of John. Its 'high christology' is not intrinsically an offence against Jewish monotheism. Philo, the Jewish philosopher of religion, knows the 'Logos' as a 'second God' alongside God, and the notion that this Logos took the form of human beings and angels was familiar to him. However, for Philo it would have been inconceivable that this Logos became incarnate exclusively in a single individual, He would not have said that heaven is fully present on earth. That is precisely what the Johannine Christ claims for himself. Also as the earthly one, the Johannine Jesus says that he is one with God (10.30; 17.11, 21). That provokes the repudiation of the Johannine Jews. When after a healing on the sabbath Jesus claims that he is continuing the works of his Father they want to kill him, because he has made himself equal with God (5.18). It offends them that a human being *makes* himself God on his own initiative. The conflict over the high christology occurs once again after the shepherd discourse. After Jesus says 'I and the Father are one' (10.30), the Johannine Jews attempt to stone him. There is no mistaking the fact that in the Gospel of John (and in the living reality of the Johannine community) the high christology has become a point of dispute between Jews and Christians. In Paul and the synoptics there was no trace of this dispute. But by this very recognition of the unity of Jesus with God the Gospel of John seeks to lead to a higher stage of understanding – beyond the synoptics and Paul – and thus deepens the schism between Jews and Christians in the biblical religion.

The prologue contains the programme of such a 'hermeneutic in stages' as a guide to reading the whole gospel. It begins immediately with God. The origin of all things is present in the revealer. He comes directly from the heart of the Father and alone brings authentic knowledge of God. No one else has seen God (1.18). The whole of reality is a hidden 'Word' which is meant by him and 'expressed' in him. For this 'Word' has created all things. It existed before everything else. Moses and John the Baptist have their light and their truth from it.

Knowledge of the Word takes place in two stages. They correspond to the two strophes of the prologue (1.1–13, 14–18). Both begin with a statement about the Word (= the Logos), John 1.1 with 'In the beginning was the Word, and the Word was with God', John 1.14 with 'And the Word became flesh and dwelt among us and we have seen his glory'. The first strophe is formulated predominantly in the third person singular, the second predominantly in the first person plural. John the Baptist appears in both strophes. The statements referring to him were probably inserted by the evangelist, since their prosaic nature distinguishes them from the hymnic prose which surrounds them. John the Baptist has to appear twice, because the faith which he is to create by his testimony is developed in two stages, as the following schematic survey shows:

| | |
|---|---|
| 1–5 | The creation of the world by the Logos, who was with God from the beginning. The failure of the darkness to understand his light. |
| *6–8* | *John the Baptist's testimony to the light: all are to come to faith through this testimony.* |
| 9–11 | The rejection of the light and |
| 12–13 | the acceptance of the light among those who 'believe' in his name. |

| | |
|---|---|
| 14–18 | The revelation of God by the Logos in the flesh and the vision of his glory. |
| *15* | *The testimony of John the Baptist to Jesus' pre-existence: Jesus exists before John the Baptist.* |
| 16–17 | Moses and the law are surpassed by the revelation of 'grace and truth'. |
| 18 | The authentic revelation of God by the one who is the 'only-begotten God'. |

It is easy to recognize the following 'stages': 1. The first strophe speaks of 'believing', the second of 'seeing'. 2. The first testimony of John the Baptist speaks of the light, the second of pre-existence. 3. In the first strophe the light illuminates all human beings and is accepted by children of God. In the second strophe the glory of God is accessible only to a 'we-circle'.

It is also clear that the whole prologue depicts a way from not-understanding to understanding. 1.5 says: 'The darkness did not understand (or grasp) it (the light).' At the end complete understanding is possible: 'The only one who has divine being has proclaimed him (God).' As no one has seen God, God is first made accessible through him.

What is the aim of this hermeneutics in stages? At first glance one could say that it is focused on belief in the pre-existent Christ, with which the Gospel of John goes beyond the belief in Christ to be found in the synoptic gospels. But what is decisive is the way in which the new Christian religion gives itself a foundation and legitimation from its christological centre. The internal autonomy of the Christian faith, the way in which it is defined by its own subject, is the aim of the Johannine hermeneutics by stages. Everything is to be governed by Christ. And all light in the world comes from him – whether the light in the cosmos, references in the scriptures or the human hunger for life. The one who has created all things is at work in everything.

This hermeneutics in stages stamps the structure of the Gospel of John. The revelation takes place in two stages, which correspond to its two parts. The public activity of the revealer (John 1 – 12) is surpassed by a revelation in the circle of disciples (John 13 – 17, 20 – 21). But we also find progress in knowledge and understanding within the two parts. In the public part the reader of the Gospel of John time and again takes the step from an initial faith orientated on the visible to belief in the revelation of the invisible. Thus the miracles of Jesus are interpreted symbolically and the sayings of Jesus take on a deeper sense through a misunderstanding. The same goes for the revelation in the circle of disciples in the second part of the Gospel of John, which is not public. A first farewell discourse is followed by a second, which treats the themes of the first discourse at a higher level. This re-reading of preceding texts comes to a climax in the high-priestly prayer (John 17), in which once again the whole mission of Jesus is interpreted in retrospect.

In the first part of the Gospel of John Jesus time and again coincides with human expectations of salvation which he fulfils and surpasses at the same time. The critical approach to the traditional honorific names begins in the very first chapter of the Gospel of John. The first disciples are directed to Jesus by John the Baptist. They come to him and gain further disciples, because they see the traditional expectation of the redeemer fulfilled in him. They have found the 'messiah' (1.41). Nathanael confesses Jesus as 'Son of God' (1.49). Whereas in the synoptic gospels the disciples only penetrate with great difficulty to the knowledge of the dignity of Jesus, in the Gospel of John they have this knowledge from the beginning. But here they represent only a first stage of knowledge. Jesus (in his answer to Nathanael's confession) promises yet more: '"You shall see greater things than these." And he said to him, "Truly, truly, you shall see heaven opened, and the angels of God ascending and descending upon the Son of Man"' (1.50–51). All expectations are surpassed by a 'seeing'. The 'greater' that the disciples will see – at the second stage of the Johannine hermeneutics in stages – is the direct unity of Jesus with the heavenly world.

Thus Jesus is not yet fully known if his dignity is expressed with the traditional honorific titles like 'Christ' and 'Son of God', and the expectations of a redeemer denoted by them are seen as being fulfilled in him. The decisive thing is how the redeemer defines himself. He does this in the 'I am' sayings, in which the christology tied to titles is surpassed by a christology in images: I am the bread of life, the light of the world, the door, the good shepherd, the resurrection and the life, etc. These images follow a deliberate order. The first 'I am' saying about the bread of life invites people to *come* to Jesus (6.35); the second, about the light of the world, calls on them to *follow* Jesus (8.12). Those who do so cross a threshold which leads to a new world. Therefore the third saying emphasizes the character of the existence of discipleship as a threshold: whoever follows Jesus (10.4) and *enters* through the door, enters a new sphere of life (10.9). In this sphere he is protected by the good shepherd of whom the fourth 'I am' saying speaks (10.11). What he finds in this new sphere of life is stated by the last 'I am' saying in the public part: Jesus is the resurrection and the life. Whoever *believes* in him has life not just as future life but as present reality. In all these images the revealer defines himself in a way which transcends the traditional roles of redeemer and revealer.

Thus in the public part of his activity Jesus is confronted with the world's expectation of life and salvation. By contrast, in the farewell part he grapples with the sorrow and anxiety of his disciples. He prepares them for a life in the world without him. Just as the revelation of life is the task of his public activity, so here too he has a task: the revelation of the commandment to love. He speaks explicitly of a 'new commandment' which he has to communicate (13.34). And here he could refer back to the 'first' commandment with which he summed up his message at the end of his public activity: the commandment to reveal life and make it accessible (12.49–50).

But the 'new commandment', too, is revealed in stages. This happens for the first time in the farewell speech in dialogue form (in 13.34–35); the second time in the farewell speech in monologue form (in 15.12–17). There is a reference in the text that makes this the most important statement in the Gospel of John. Previously Jesus had often proclaimed *that* he is saying what he has heard from the Father. But we never hear *what* he has heard. Only once does the gospel emphasize that Jesus has now said *everything* that he has heard from the Father, namely at the second formulation of the commandment to love:

> This is my commandment, that you love one another as I have loved you. Greater love has no man than this, that he lay down his life for his friends. You are my friends if you do what I command you. No longer do I call you servants, for the servant does not know what his master is doing, but I have called you friends, for *all* that I have heard from my Father I have made known to you. (15.12–15)

Here it is said explicitly that the command to love says everything – really everything – that Jesus has to communicate on the basis of his familiarity with the Father. The whole of the Gospel of John is written to bring the commandment to love from heaven to earth. Thus all previous revelation is superseded. For hitherto the disciples were servants in relation to God and Jesus; now they have become his friends. A religious knowledge is a decisive characteristic.

This new knowledge of God is also evident in the two 'I am' sayings in the farewell discourses. Only in them is God brought into play as Father. Jesus is first 'the way, the truth and the life', because he opens the way to the *Father* (14.6–7). Secondly he is the good vine, because the *Father* is the gardener

(15.1). If the emphasis in the first saying is on access to the Father, in the second it is on the consequence of this: there it is a matter of *coming* to God through Jesus, here of *abiding* in God. The fruit of this abiding relationship with God is love.

This love is opposed to the 'hatred' of the world. It becomes evident in persecutions, e.g. by the synagogue (16.2), to which the Gospel of John reacts with anti-Judaism. Regardless of the fact that this attitude must be rejected, it has to be interpreted historically. It is not anti-Judaism in principle. Otherwise the Gospel of John could not say 'Salvation comes from the Jews' (4.22). When the Johannine Jews seek the life of Jesus and even kill Christians in the present (16.3), in the view of the Gospel of John they are not fulfilling their own will. As free children of Abraham they would not do something like this (8.33–34). They stand under an alien will. They follow the will of Satan. But who stands behind Satan? In the Gospel of John he is called the 'ruler of the world' (12.31; 14.30; 16.11) – and indeed at some points the Romans as rulers of the world stand behind Satan.

- After Satan has entered into Judas to bring Jesus to the cross (13.27), in John 14.30 Judas is announced as 'ruler of the world' and in John 18.3 he can 'take a cohort' to arrest Jesus. In the Roman world of the time all readers knew that a cohort can only be commanded by someone with a Roman mandate. So Judas and the Roman rulers of the world belong together.

- The Jewish aristocracy puts pressure on Pilate with the argument that Jesus has made himself king. If he lets Jesus go, he will no longer be a friend of the emperor (19.12). They claim to have only one king, namely the emperor (19.15). The decisive argument against Jesus is their loyalty to the emperor. This tips the scales when it comes to killing him.

By means of such constructions the Gospel of John attempts to explain how Jesus came to be killed. It is not 'the Jews' themselves, of whom the gospel speaks far too sweepingly, who are the cause of his death, but only Jews who have become dependent on the rulers of this world. Satan is a symbolic concentration of the power of the Romans. So in the Gospel of John it is not simply that a blind 'prejudice' is being turned outwards. Rather, the opposition between Jews and Christians as the expression of a politically conditioned alienation of Judaism is being grasped with the means of mythical language. Nevertheless, Johannine anti-Judaism is to be firmly rejected because its statements are so open to misunderstanding.

The hostile world stands over against the community. The understanding of the community in the Gospel of John has time and again inspired groups which have been opposed to the church. We hear nothing of offices. However, Jesus does appoint three representatives for the time after his death: the beloved disciple, the Paraclete and Peter.

In the farewell discourses Jesus promises the *Paraclete* (= advocate, defender) as his successor. After his return to the Father he will send 'another paraclete' as his representative (14.16). In the passion section the *beloved disciple* is the only disciple who perseveres with Jesus to the end. Jesus appoints him as a representative while hanging on the cross, when he says to Mary, 'Woman, behold your son!', and to the beloved disciple, 'Behold your mother!' (19.26–27). Finally, in the Easter section *Peter* is appointed to Jesus' role as shepherd. Despite betrayal and failure he is entrusted with the task of feeding the sheep (21.15–17). His martyrdom is prophesied. The specific function of each of these representatives is decisive.

In the Gospel of John the *beloved disciple* has the task of serving as a witness to Jesus who has understood the Lord better than the other disciples. He lies in his bosom (13.23) – as Jesus lay in the bosom of the Father (1.18) – and just as Jesus is the true interpreter of the Father (1.18), so too the beloved disciple is his interpreter. His most important function for the future is to write down the Gospel of John (21.24–25). By attributing the gospel to the disciple who is superior to all others in understanding, the Gospel of John assures itself the highest rank among all attempts to write down the sayings and actions of Jesus in a book. Now it could be said that the Paraclete, too, performs the task of giving an authentic interpretation of Jesus. But there is one thing that distinguishes the beloved disciple from him: he writes. He composes a book, whereas the Paraclete speaks. With his book he gives Johannine faith a stability, so that it can also be present in the future.

In the Gospel of John the *Paraclete* is identified with the 'Holy Spirit' and the 'spirit of truth'. Like the beloved disciple, he too continues the activity of Jesus. But he does not fix what Jesus has said on papyrus. Rather, he brings new, living revelation – also over and above what Jesus said in the past. Jesus says of him: 'I have yet many things to say to you, but you cannot bear them now. When the Spirit of truth comes, he will guide you into all the truth; for he will not speak on his own authority, but whatever he hears he will speak, and he will declare to you the things that are to come' (16.12–13). The thought here is of inspired discourse. The Paraclete hands on what he has heard. He will reveal the future. Here primitive Christian prophecy is presupposed. As living discourse it supplements the revelation that is fixed in writing. It ensures the flexibility of the tradition over and above its stability, i.e. its constantly new exegesis and assimilation to future situations.

*Peter* is the last of the three successors. In contrast to the other two he is clearly demoted. The beloved disciple embodies the authentic understanding of Jesus. Peter often misunderstands his master. But he too has an indispensable function, which is indicated in his miraculous fishing trip in John 21 and directly spoken of in his appointment as good shepherd. Peter is to receive and hold together the narrative community of the Johannine sign world. He is the shepherd who holds together the Christian church. Without this social basis even the sublime Johannine theology – a bold reinterpretation of primitive Christian religion – cannot exist.

The Gospel of John is a high point in the history of the origin of primitive Christian religion. Here a new religion is organizing itself around its christological centre and becoming aware of itself. In the process it is interpreting itself once again in a fundamentally new way. This new interpretation is governed by the fact that it is facing a turning point in the history of religion. We detect in it the rise of 'gnosis', which combines three basic motifs: (1) a radical devaluation of the world as the work of a demiurge who is subordinate and is either ignorant or malicious, and who is distinguished from the true God of the other world; (2) a radical revaluation of the human self as a heavenly spark which was lost in this world; and (3) the conviction that deliverance takes place through 'gnosis', through the intuitive recognition of an identity of the human self with the God of the other world. This gnosis is a variant of mystical religion. In the Gospel of John Jesus is the only Gnostic: he is the only one who has come from heaven and knows that he is returning there (9.14). At one point the picture of the creator God almost turns into that of a Satan (8.37–47). The Gnostic temptation can be detected. But all in all the Gospel of John is a firm repudiation of it: the world has been created by the redeemer himself (1.1ff.). And human beings cannot satisfy their longing from God by the knowledge that inwardly they are identical with God. On the contrary, in the first farewell discourse Philip asks Jesus about the fulfilment of the longing for the vision of God. And he is given the answer: 'Have I been with you so long, and yet you do not know me, Philip? He who has seen me has seen the Father' (14.9). In Christ the God whom no one has yet seen becomes visible (1.18). In him the God of the other world touches the earth. But the temptation to Gnosticism which is already detectable in the Gospel of John had a further effect. The Johannine letters bear witness to the controversies into which they drove the Johannine groups.

## The Johannine letters

Just as the letters generally are earlier than the gospels, so too the Johannine letters could be earlier than the Gospel of John. But in the Johannine circle the development was probably the other way round, from the gospel to the letters. For in the Gospel of John we find a clear confrontation with Judaism, whereas in the Johannine letters it has disappeared. The letters are about controversies with the world – Jews are not mentioned anywhere – and about conflicts within Christianity over the understanding of Christ. These conflicts, too, are the effects of a consistent monotheism: if the one and only God is thought of consistently as other-worldly, then it is hard to imagine how he could make concrete contact with the earth. Now precisely that was a central statement of the Gospel of John: 'The Logos (God's reason) became flesh' (John 1.14). In the gnosis which first began around that time the other-worldliness of God was yet further heightened, and the world was additionally devalued as a place of evil. Consequently it was even harder to understand how in Christ God and world came together. Rather, it was natural to say that the deity had associated with an earthly human being only in transitory fashion, to separate from it again before death. In 1 John such 'docetism' has led to a split in the community. Here tendencies already indicated in the Gospel of John are taken further by Gnostic 'dissidents'. These dissidents understood themselves as a group which had gone beyond normal Christianity: as those who have 'gone ahead' (cf. 2 John 9). In their way they present the programme of a Johannine hermeneutic in stages.

*(a) 1 John*

In this situation 1 John gives a new interpretation of Johannine theology in which its bold features are somewhat retracted. There is a stronger emphasis on futuristic eschatology: 'It does not yet appear what we shall be' (1 John 3.2). 1 John 2.28 expects the traditional 'parousia'. The doctrine of the Paraclete – of the spirit who leads beyond the teaching of Jesus – is reformulated: Jesus himself is the only Paraclete in heaven (2.1). Therefore the spirit cannot be separated from Jesus. Rather, belief in the real incarnation becomes the criterion of true faith: 'Every spirit which confesses that Jesus Christ has come in the flesh is of God' (4.2). 1 John was written to make the bold Gospel of John acceptable to a wider Christianity – and to this end it distances itself from radical groups in the Johannine circle. Above all the notion of love is brought to bear against them as an appeal to the unity of the

community. Here remarkably the command to love is introduced both as a 'new commandment' and also as an 'old
commandment which you had from the beginning' (2.7). In
my view this presupposes the Gospel of John, which spoke of
a 'new commandment'. It has either to be corrected (since
the commandment to love is already contained in the Old
Testament) or interpreted (for Jesus' new commandment is
already an old tradition for the Johannine community). That
makes all the more urgent the question why 1 John nowhere
quotes the Gospel of John. 1 John is meant to be read as a
letter written by the one who has composed the Gospel of
John or who comes from the circle of the disciples. Granted,
it does not name an author, but it does emphasize 'that which
was from the beginning, which we have heard, which we have
seen with our eyes, which we have looked upon and touched
with our hands, concerning the word of life, that we proclaim'
(1 John 1.1). Here an eyewitness, indeed someone who has
had bodily contact with Jesus, wants to speak – like the beloved
disciple who lay on Jesus' 'breast' (13.23; 21.20), or Thomas,
who was allowed to touch the Risen Christ with his hands
(20.27). Had 1 John quoted the Gospel of John as an alien
book it could not have sustained this suggestion. The normal
reader would spontaneously distinguish the author of 1 John
from the author of the Gospel of John. But not the historical-
critical reader. Despite the same style and a related theology
it is possible to recognize clear differences between the Gospel
of John and 1 John. To mention just one: the Gospel of John
limits itself to Christ in mystical-sounding sayings. By contrast
1 John knows a God mysticism: 'God is love, and he who abides
in love abides in God, and God abides in him' (4.16).

### (b)  2 and 3 John

The two short letters of John give us insights into the everyday
side of the controversy in the Johannine circle. In them we
hear a 'presbyter' speaking as author. This will not be the
designation of a primitive Christian office which by then was
already widespread, since there is no reference to such offices
in the Johannine letters. Rather, the 'elder' (the *presbyteros*) is

meant to be a charismatic figure who owes his nickname to his age. It has time and again been conjectured that he is identical with the author of 1 John or even the last redaction of the Gospel of John, but that cannot be substantiated.

In 2 John he forbids the community he addresses to accept itinerant false teachers. Belief in the incarnation is mentioned as a criterion. There are people who want to go beyond the normal faith of the community (2 John 9). The demarcation is made with an iron consistency: 'If any one comes to you and does not bring this doctrine, do not receive him into the house or give him any greeting, for he who greets him shares his wicked work' (2 John 10–11). If the greeting were the 'holy kiss' (cf. 1 Cor. 16.20), that would be tolerable. But if it is a matter of respect generally, here we could see the potential for inquisition in the Johannine 'theology of love'.

So in reading 3 John the modern reader feels a certain satisfaction that the author is experiencing what he has imputed to others: his messengers have been rejected by a community leader named Diotrephes. But they were welcomed in the house of Gaius. Probably Diotrephes and his followers saw themselves as orthodox representatives of Christianity and were defending themselves against the infiltration of a group whose theology was in fact very bold. The messengers of the 'elder' will in turn have understood themselves with the same justification as representatives of true Christianity. Structurally this is a conflict between local authorities in settled communities and itinerant charismatics. 3 John shows that the decision was increasingly made in favour of the local authorities. This led to jealousy within the community: Diotrephes does not have at least Gaius and his circle under his control. And he demonstrates his independence.

## The Apocalypse of John

The Apocalypse, or Revelation, of John was first included among the Johannine writings in the course of the formation of the canon. Its author, the primitive Christian prophet John who was banished to the island of Patmos, was identified with the evangelist John at a secondary stage. This identification was not just made possible by the same name. Rather, in John 21.2–3 the author is associated with an intense imminent expectation: there is a rumour that he will experience the coming of the Lord. This expectation can be read out of the end of the Apocalypse of John. There Jesus promises, 'Yes, I will come quickly' (22.20). The imminent expectation that the Gospel of John has left far behind with its present eschatology flares up once again in the Apocalypse of John. In the Gospel of John and in the Apocalypse of John we therefore find ourselves in different worlds. If they were written by the same author, he would have to have experienced a complete break in his thought and language. So even in the early church there were doubts about his identity.

John and a circle of primitive Christian prophets around him (cf. 22.9) probably came from Palestine. The Roman-Jewish war (AD 66–74) had stamped their experience. Revelation 11.1–2 quotes a prophecy which could come from the end of the Jewish war, when the temple forecourt had already been captured by the enemy and the Jews in the inner temple were still hoping for a divine miracle. The prophetic circle behind the Apocalypse has experienced the Roman empire as an annihilating power. And that has an effect on its fears and hopes. The war has driven it to Asia Minor. The imagery of apocalyptic is familiar to it. In an introductory vision of Jesus the seer is given the task of writing down 'what is and what will happen hereafter' (1.19). He performs the first task in the letters to the churches, in which he addresses problems of the present; the second in several cycles of visions from Rev. 4ff. onwards.

The situation of the churches emerges from the seven letters which the prophet sends to them (2.1 – 3.22). For example in Pergamon and Thyatira he is fighting against 'Nicolaitans' and adherents of a prophetess Jezebel. He accuses both of immorality and eating meat offered to idols (Rev. 2.14–15; 2.20). Here he could mean Christians who claimed the Pauline freedom to eat meat offered to idols and did not see that they were to reduce their contact with the pagan world. The seer seeks to drive a wedge between these

Christians and the world – also by demonizing the world. For alongside the internal front there is an external front: the Roman empire.

The conflict with the empire is introduced by a great vision of God's throne room. This is a counter-scene to the throne room of the emperor. The way in which God is addressed in it as 'our Lord and God' (Rev. 4.11) seems like a deliberate contrast to the way in which Domitian was addressed as *dominus et deus*. At all events the conflict between God and the power of the world is the great theme of the Apocalypse of John. It is waged by the 'lamb', which in the Apocalypse is a symbol of Christ. It is the slaughtered lamb, a sacrifice. But only this lamb is capable of opening the book with the seven seals.

The book of the end of history is opened: it contains nightmarish images of eschatological plagues arranged in cycles according to seven seals, seven trumpets and seven bowls. Time and again the same events take place before our eyes, but time and again they are depicted differently. Satan has been thrown out of heaven, so he now rages all the more on earth 'because he knows that he has only a little time' (12.12). The target of his anger is a woman with a child; they stand for the church. Two further monsters disclose what the conflict is about: Christians see themselves exposed to the propaganda for the emperor cult. There has already been a martyr, Antipas, in Pergamon (2.13). However, there can be no talk of a great persecution. The prophet John is an example of this. For he has got off lightly with banishment. His view of the world is stamped, not by experiences of persecution, but by expectations of persecution. Precisely because of that one must admire his great sensitivity. He has seen more clearly than any New Testament author the incompatibility of a state which exalts itself in religious terms with Christianity – at a time when there were relatively few conflicts. This prophet has the true power of a seer: already in the first century he foresees the great persecutions of Christians which began only in the third and fourth centuries. For him the Roman state is a monster rising from the sea (13.1–10). In mythical images he indicates that it is not the political power but those who venerate it who are the problem. So he makes a second monster emerge from the earth: the representatives of the imperial cult in Asia Minor. They are just as bad as the emperor in Rome! Power is given its pernicious force only by human assent. Here the seer rightly sees the cause of the Christians' difficulties. All this best fits the time of Domitian, i.e. the first half of the 90s, when his cult in Asia Minor was enforced by the local aristocracies there. This put the Christians in a difficult situation. Nevertheless we can say that it is not the Roman empire which has declared war on the Christians; rather, a primitive Christian prophet has declared war on the Roman empire. He sees it as the incarnation of Satan. Rome appears once again – transparently – in the role of the whore of Babylon, who 'was drunk with the blood of saints' (17.6); it will perish with all its economic and political power. At the end (from 10.11 – 22.5) there are visions of the consummation of God's plan in history: a great vision of the thousand-year kingdom that comes before the final kingdom in which the messiah will reign together with the martyrs – the original model of all 'chiliastic' currents (chiliastic = thousand-year) (Rev. 20). After this a new heaven and a new earth will come. Then God will dwell with human beings: 'He will wipe all tears from their eyes: death will be no more, neither sorrow, nor crying, nor pain' (21.4).

The great theme of the Apocalypse of John is God's establishment of himself in the face of all his adversaries – especially the political and economic power of Rome. Whereas others at that time were developing the feeling that Rome would last for ever – *Roma aeterna* – here we have an insight into a small culture which expected the collapse of mighty Rome. Rome appears as a bloodthirsty beast. The aggression expressed in the streams of blood in these visions may be terrifying – but these are streams of blood caused by a political power which has made itself absolute. And to this is opposed the blood of the lamb who 'was slain' by this very power. That early Christianity accepted this rebellious writing into its canon (although there were objections to it in the East) shows the tremendous potential for indignation that a demonstratively unmilitant subculture can have. This is understandable and in my view also justified in view of the excesses of absolutist power, even if (like many in the early church) we shrink from the violent aggression of its images.

It remains a riddle why this writing and the Johannine writings form a group. The final redaction of the canon understood all five Johannine writings as a unity and attributed them to the same author, the apostle John. We also find some motifs which bind them together: the motif of the water of life (Rev. 7.16–17; 21.6; John 4.10ff.), the designation 'word of God' (Rev. 19.13; John 1.1) and 'lamb of God' for Jesus (Rev. 5.6, etc.; John 1.29). In both the concept of 'witness' plays an important role. And yet the two writings are diametrically opposed to each other: the Apocalypse expresses religious aggressiveness in explosive images, the Gospel of John advocates a theology of love which would best like to withdraw into a close circle of friends. What binds the two together, though, is the history of the circles who handed them down. Behind the Apocalypse stands a group of primitive Christian prophets who had fled from Palestine to Asia Minor. It contains Palestinian traditions, but these are given their final form only in Asia Minor. The same is true of the Gospel of John. This gospel may have been formulated in Syria (at least in its first version); it was perhaps given its final form in Asia Minor and there supplemented with letters. It likewise presupposes that a group brought its theology from East to West in the neighbourhood around Ephesus. We also know of other primitive Christian groups which fled to Asia (probably in view of the Jewish war). They include Philip, the missionary of Samaria, who was buried with his daughters in Asia Minor (*CH* III 31, 3 = V 24, 2). Papias attests further tradents of Jesus traditions for Asia Minor – who certainly also include people from Palestine (*CH* III 39, 4). These exiles brought very different theologies with them, but 'abroad' they were regarded as a group, and perhaps despite their great theological differences they felt that they belonged together. Moreover because of their common fate they in fact developed some common features.

1. In terms of literary history we note a convergence: in 1–3 John the group behind the Gospel of John adopted

the letter form which was already recognized in Asia Minor on the basis of the Pauline mission. The same happened in the group behind the Apocalypse: at a secondary stage, in the seven letters to the churches it formulated primitive Christian prophetic sayings in the letter form recognized in Asia Minor (Rev. 2.1 – 3.22). And it also gives the Apocalypse a letter framework by the way in which it shapes the beginning and the end.

2. Despite all the oppositions, the theology of the Apocalypse and the Gospel of John have a common feature: their opposition to the world. In the Gospel of John it appears as a 'metaphysical' dualism between light and darkness, truth and lie, God and Satan; in the Apocalypse as a power struggle between the Roman empire and the community enciphered in myth. The Roman empire is Satan himself. We can see why emigrants should develop dualistic interpretations of the world. The specific features that they give these interpretations can be very different.

3. There are parallels in church constitutions. Both groups bring a very archaic community order to regions in which there were already bishops and presbyters. In his letters the apocalyptist interferes in the communities, passing over these authorities. The evangelist John ignores the authorities in his image of the vine, in which there is no place for a bishop between grapes and stem; all Christians are directly in Christ. The presbyter directly addresses Diotrephes, a leader of the community, in 3 John.

4. The different groups of emigrants gathered all the more around their charismatics. We can recognize three historical figures: John the apocalyptist, Philip the evangelist and the presbyter of the Johannine letters. The anonymous figure of the 'beloved disciple' is hard to grasp. It could unite historical features of all three charismatics and to this degree be a literary construction aimed at claiming superiority to all other already recognized apostles and authorities by a single

point of reference. But experiences with historical figures have certainly found their way into it. The beloved disciple is a disciple of Jesus, as Philip is. Philip mediates access to Jesus for (godfearing) Gentiles as in John 12.20ff. In Asia Minor, Philip was regarded as a priest – just as the beloved disciple in the Gospel of John appears as a relative of the high priest (John 18.16). According to John 21.20–23 the expectation is attached to him that he will not die but experience the parousia. That recalls the imminent expectation in the Apocalypse, where Jesus promises the seer, 'I am coming soon' (Rev. 22.12). This could have given rise to the rumour that the seer would experience the parousia. This beloved disciple (like Peter) survives many other authorities. That recalls the '*presbyteros*', whose honorific title 'the elder' attests the length of his life.

So if in the second century the editors of the canon regarded the Johannine writings as a unitary group despite their different character, these writings could have contained recollections of emigrant groups from Syria and Palestine who had shaped the history of primitive Christianity towards the end of the first century AD. Geographically they formed a connection between the focal points of earliest primitive Christianity. Following the domination in the first generation of the East with its centres in Jerusalem and Antioch, and a shift to Rome and Asia Minor with the Pauline mission, after AD 70, as a result of migratory movements, new impulses penetrated the West from the Syrian and Palestinian regions of primitive Christianity: the Johannine groups brought to Asia Minor a theology close to Gnosticism, which strongly stamped the Christianity there. The Gospel of John could supplement the abstract picture of Jesus in the letters of Paul and bring it to life. Alongside it the apocalyptic theology of the Apocalypse of John also left traces, although it never seems to have been as widely accepted as the Gospel of John. Around the same time a reinforced and transformed Jewish Christianity brought its ethical theology to the West as far as Rome. The Gospel of Matthew is the main witness to this. In Rome it is already the most frequently quoted Gospel in Justin. The letter of James and the Didache are also secondary testimonies to this Jewish Christianity after AD 70, except that these two writings spread far more slowly in the West. James is attested for the first time in Origen, i.e. in the East, but found its way into the canon. The Didache remained outside the canon and is similarly attested above all for the East by an Oxyrhynchus papyrus, a Coptic translation preserved in fragments and the Apostolic Constitutions.

# CHAPTER 9

# The Way to the 'New Testament' as a Literary Unity

The New Testament is the result of a process in three phases. First comes a *fellowship with oral communication*: of the traditions of Jesus and the preaching of the apostles. Oral traditions can still be recognized in the brief pericopes of the gospels, each of which could have been handed down independently, and in the formulae and confessions of the letters, in which fragments of the language of the first Christians have been preserved for us. Such oral traditions continued to live on even after they were set down in writing. Papias in the second century still knew oral tradition about Jesus and prized the 'living and abiding testimony' more than any book (*CH* III 39, 4). The literature of the first generation of primitive Christianity, the letters of Paul and Q, is still rooted in a fellowship of oral communication: Q fixes the oral tradition of itinerant charismatics; as a travelling missionary Paul replaces his personal presence by letters. Only Romans crosses the threshold to more formal writing. But it too is not yet fully detached from Paul's life: he will visit those to whom he is writing. His written communication remains embedded in an oral culture. However, Romans was already written with a view to a time when Paul would possibly no longer be alive. It is 'Paul's testament', which seeks to have an effect even apart from the author's presence.

In the second phase of the history of primitive Christian literature a *closed literary fellowship* formed within the communities. The period from around AD 70 and AD 120 is the heyday of primitive Christian literature. Most of the writings of the New Testament were written at this time. The pseudepigraphical letters were added to the authentic letters of Paul. From the start they came into being as a result of intertextual references to those on which they were modelled. They cannot be imagined without an intensive use of the authentic letters of Paul. In the gospel literature earlier writings are used as sources. Written sources must have been worked over even in the Gospel of Mark. At least the synoptic apocalypse (Mark 13) and the passion story are based on written sources. The Gospels of Matthew and Luke use Q and Mark. Gospels are presupposed in the Gospel of John, without being taken over as sources. Thus both letters and gospels attest a dense play with intertextual references to written texts at this time, which means an amazing literary exchange between the communities.

The intertextuality which can be detected everywhere shows how the primitive Christian literature which arose after AD 70 deliberately or in fact had the function of correcting the tradition. In the first generation Christianity had quickly spread to the West. But there it had been stamped by an outsider who was not representative of primitive Christianity, Paul. He had not only rushed round the world but had also left behind an impressive letter literature. The primitive Christian writers who follow him are concerned to correct the influence of this prominent outsider and to compensate for his domination. Here on the one hand Paul's school corrects itself, and on the other two new impulses come from the East: Johannine primitive Christianity and a new ethical Jewish Christianity.

- In the pseudepigrapha of the New Testament there is no mistaking the fact that the Deutero-Pauline letters imitate Paul in order to correct him. Ephesians and the Pastorals seek to create a Paul who can be used by the church, who is less combative and less controversial, but also less charismatic and unruly than the authentic Paul. The Catholic letters in turn seek to compensate for his domination by revaluing other authorities of primitive Christianity over against him: James the brother of the Lord and Jude, and the apostles Peter, John and James. Acts can also be understood as a correction of the image of Paul.

- In the Gospel of John Johannine Christianity offers a new interpretation of Christian faith for Christians who are dissatisfied with the simple faith of ordinary Christians. It corrects the simpler synoptic Christianity with a more subtle pneumatic picture of Christ. The Apocalypse is a protest against a Christianity which conforms too much to the world and abruptly corrects tendencies to assimilate to this world which are spreading in the communities of Asia Minor. Coming from the East, both spread in regions which were the focal point of the Pauline mission, namely in Ephesus and its surroundings.

- The Jewish Christianity of the Gospel of Matthew (along with the letter of James and the Didache) deliberately introduces a Christianity concentrated on the ethical into regions which Paul had originally won for Christianity. A radical religion of redemption trusting only in the grace of God is here corrected by a Christianity of practical discipleship. Its practical and moral Christianity had to find an echo in the West as far as Rome – and in its matter-of-fact basic structure corresponds to some writings produced there, like 1 Clement and the Shepherd of Hermas, though these are not theologically related to Matthaean Christianity.

A second characteristic over and above the strong intertextual network of these writings of primitive Christianity is the growing degree of independence of the texts from oral communication. The pseudepigraphical letters seek to detach the letters from any living interaction. They deliberately veil the intention of their real authors to communicate with those who are being addressed and attribute them to a fictitious author who has meanwhile died, and who was writing to quite a different audience. Pseudepigraphical writings are literature from the start. But the gospels, too, seek to be self-sufficient as depictions of the life and teaching of Jesus. Time and again the Gospel of Mark refers to 'the teaching of Jesus' as if it wanted to quote only extracts from it (cf. Mark 4.2), or announces 'parables' in the plural, only to produce just one (12.1ff.). Here we can still trace how it is embedded in a wider oral tradition. But the Gospel of Matthew already sets out to bring together all the teaching of Jesus that Christians need 'until the end of the world'. It seeks to give a self-sufficient depiction of Jesus. And Luke–Acts suggests even more that in contrast to its still incomplete predecessor it now finally wants to give a comprehensive description of the beginnings of Christianity. The Gospel of John certainly concedes that there are many more Jesus traditions than those written down in it, and does not set out to suppress the other gospels, but through the beloved disciple it does want exclusively to be the authentic testimony to the truth that is sufficient for salvation (cf. John 20.30–31; 21.24–25).

This literature which is closely woven together intertextually continues in the apostolic fathers: the letters of Ignatius of Antioch are an echo of the letters of Paul; the letter of Polycarp feels like a collage of New Testament statements, and so on. The intertextual references in this period are still limited to the primitive Christian writings. The primitive Christianity which has newly come into being certainly forms a literary fellowship, but it still does not address the outside world, and in content, too, takes up few of its notions: the quotation from Aratus in Acts 17.28 or the myth of the phoenix as an image of the resurrection in 1 Clem. 25 are exceptions. All in all, it draws its content from its own traditions, which go back to the Jewish Bible, to Jesus and the apostles.

In a third phase, which we cannot demarcate precisely from the previous one, the picture in the second century becomes more diverse. Primitive Christianity becomes a *literary fellowship which is opening up*. The primitive Christian writings develop in three directions:

1. The forms coined for communication within the communities are continued in the so-called *apocrypha* and

*apostolic fathers*: the latter are writings which are not attributed to the 'apostles' but to their descendants. They are primitive Christian in form and content: the letters of Ignatius and Clement, the letters of Barnabas and Polycarp and the Shepherd of Hermas, and the Teaching of the Apostles (the Didache). Others are included among the 'apocrypha' (the 'hidden writings'). They include all the other primitive Christian writings which continue New Testament forms and themes, e.g. the Gospel of Thomas or the Jewish-Christian gospels. In some of these apocrypha we find openness to pagan forms and content. The Acts of the Apostles take over elements from the ancient romance, the discourses of the disciples with the Risen Christ take over elements of ancient dialogue literature. The Gnostic writings take in Platonic notions (see below).

2.  In this period, for the first time an early Christian literature comes into being which is deliberately addressed to the outside world, in order to promote the undertanding of Christians there, namely *apologetic*. Quadratus in Asia Minor and Aristides in Athens sent the emperor Hadrian a written defence of Christianity. Justin's two apologies were written in Rome (between 150 and 165). The 'Discourse to the Greeks' of his pupil Tatian and the petition for the Christians by Athenagoras of Athens, etc., are also apologetic. Among the apologists Christianity appears as a reasonable cause: the Logos which has become incarnate in Christ is part of the reason of the world, which is present everywhere as seeds. Socrates and Abraham were anonymous Christians before Christ. With these writings early Christianity takes over literary forms from the environment deliberately in order to communicate with it. So we can date the end of primitive Christianity and the beginning of patristic literature (= the literature of the church fathers), as F. Overbeck did, with the apologists.

3.  Quite a different opening up to the environment takes place in the *Gnostic literature* which flourished in the

second century. These works are not addressed to the public but to small circles in Christianity in which a new interpretation of Christian faith is developed, inspired by philosophical notions. Christian teachers want to show that the Christian message is a superior philosophy of revelation for initiates. They want to communicate redemptive 'knowledge' (= gnosis). The notion of the demiurge, the creator of the world, is taken from the Platonic tradition; he is distinguished from the true other-worldly God, because this world can only have been made by an ignorant or defective god.

In this third phase primitive Christianity developed into a literary fellowship communicating with the outside world – either by addressing the public directly or by addressing educated people in Gnostic conventicles who formed inner circles within the community. This early Christian literature which opened up to its environment in its forms highlights the character of the first New Testament writings increasingly clearly – as a literature which still draws completely on primitive Christianity's own traditions. It begins to stand apart from all the other literary products of primitive Christianity. It is no longer just worked on or taken up in intertextual allusions but is quoted, so that we can make a clear distinction between a writing which quotes and a writing which is quoted. Where these writings are introduced as an authority and are cited like the Old Testament, they appear as 'canonical' scriptures, i.e. as part of the collection of writings which is normative for the communities. The two earliest examples of this are 2 Clem. 2.4 and Barn. 4.14, where sayings of Jesus are quoted as 'scripture' like the Old Testament. The criteria for belonging to the canonical collection of scriptures were apostolic origin and agreement with Christian convictions. But it was open which scriptures should belong to the canon.

The stimulus to clarifying this question was provided by the theologian Marcion, who was active in Rome around 140. Marcion had been influenced by Gnostic notions, but took them beyond the narrow circle of Gnostic conventicles by simplifying them and putting them forward with prophetic weight. He made a distinction between the God of righteousness, who had revealed himself in the Old Testament, and the unknown God of love, who reveals himself in Christ. For him the Old Testament could not be the Bible of the Christians; it had to be replaced by a collection of writings in which the revelation of the God of love was maintained. Only in Paul did he find a clear recognition of the opposition between the old revelation and the new. So his canon consisted of the Gospel of Luke (i.e. the gospel of a disciple of Paul) and ten letters of Paul (without the Pastorals); he assumed that the Gospel of Luke and the letters of Paul were full of secondary interpolations. Judaizing opponents of Paul had falsified them. So his canon rests on a text purged by literary criticism. However, Marcion could not stay in the church and hold these ideas, so he founded a church of his own.

In reaction to Marcion, primitive Christianity agreed on a canon which deliberately affirmed a greater plurality of the writings collected in it and of their content. Here we must note that Marcion was not a revolutionary when he chose only one gospel. Most communities had only one. In Syria the one-gospel principle was so deeply rooted that the four gospels could become established there only as Tatian's gospel harmony, the Diatessaron (= four as one). But since the heretic Marcion had chosen only one gospel, the recognition of four gospels became the sign of orthodoxy. Since Marcion recognized only one apostle, the Catholic letters (i.e. the letters of other apostles and brothers of the Lord) were now recognized as a balance to Paul. Since Marcion rejected the Old Testament as a basis for the community (while fully recognizing its validity for Jews), the Old Testament was now deliberately kept as the Bible of Christians. Here Marcion served as a catalyst for developments which were taking place in any case.

Where was the formation of the canon stimulated? Since Marcion was active in Rome around AD 140, a process of clarifying the canon could have begun there. 2 Peter already knows important parts of the canon (see below). Through it we get a glimpse of the development towards the formation of the canon. Since 2 Peter is stylized as Peter's testament and Peter died a martyr death in Rome, 2 Peter can only think of Rome as the place of his testament – regardless of where the letter was in fact written. Be this as it may, the earliest reference to the four gospels appears in Justin, who was active in Rome (*Dial.* 103.8). So Rome was involved in the formation of the canon. But traditions from Asia Minor as well as traditions from Rome also found their way into the canon: the Gospel of John with its Easter chronology, which was popular in Asia Minor, was put alongside the synoptic gospels. The Apocalypse of John and the Pastorals likewise point to Asia Minor. Papias of Hierapolis in Asia Minor knows the Gospel of Mark and the logia source (or the Gospel of Matthew). Therefore we can advance the hypothesis that above all those writings entered the canon on which the Christian communities in Asia Minor and Rome could agree. By contrast Syria and Palestine, the core countries of primitive Christianity in the first century, lay outside the formation of the canon. In the second century the centre of primitive Christianity had shifted, among other things because of Paul's mission to the West. The first centres of Jerusalem and Antioch were replaced by Rome and Ephesus. Accordingly, writings which had been written in Syria were now relocated 'westwards': according to Irenaeus the Gospel of Mark was written in Rome, the Gospel of John in Ephesus. Rome and Ephesus attracted gospels to themselves at a secondary stage because meanwhile they had become the strongest centres of Christianity. By contrast, other writings from Syrian Christianity like the Didache or the Jewish-Christian gospels did not find their way into the canon. They had no supporters in the decisive centres of Asia Minor and Rome.

How could the New Testament be recognized? We find two peculiarities in all Christian manuscripts: with few exceptions, all manuscripts consist not of scrolls but of codices. The Christians disseminated their writings in a form which was still unusual for the literature of the time. One could see this as a deliberate demarcation from Judaism, whose holy scriptures were handed on as scrolls. Secondly, all Christian manuscripts of the Bible (including the manuscripts of the Old Testament) are marked by abbreviations which above all embraced the *nomina sacra* for God, Christ and the Spirit. Thus ΘΕΟΣ (THEOS = God) was abbreviated as ΘΣ. These abbreviations appear in both the Old Testament and the New. They could be interpreted as a rejection of Marcion. The unity of God in the Old and New Testaments was emphasized even in the way in which the divine names were written. To this extent the nearness to the Old Testament and Judaism was emphasized.

When was the canon formed? If Marcion acted as a catalyst, this must have been between *c.* 140 and 180. For around AD 180 Irenaeus developed the first 'theory of the canon': the idea of a closed canon of the Old Testament and the New. For him creation (Old Testament) and redemption (New Testament) belong together. Redemption is the restoration of creation. That is an answer to Marcion, who contrasted the creator God and the redeemer God as two deities. Moreover, for Irenaeus the canon of four gospels is a necessity, like the four ages of the world, the four points of the compass and the four seasons. There is no corresponding reflection on the inner cohesion of the letters. Only in the case of the gospels is the canon closed; in the other parts it could still be open.

This openness still appears in Eusebius in the fourth century. He distinguished three categories of writings in respect of their recognition as being canonical, though he applies these categories very flexibly (*CH* III 25,1–7):

1. Twenty-two writings belong to the *homologoumena*, i.e. the books which are generally recognized: four gospels; fourteen letters of Paul (including Hebrews, which was disputed in the West); of the Catholic letters only 1 Peter and 1 John; and the Apocalypse (though he points out that this too is disputed).

2. The *antilegomena* are books which are disputed, but recognized by most members of the church. They comprise five Catholic letters: James, Jude, 2 Peter and 2/3 John.

3.  Among the *notha*, i.e. false books, Eusebius includes the
    Acts of Paul, the Shepherd of Hermas, the Apocalypse
    of Peter, the Letter of Barnabas, the Didache, and the
    Gospel of the Hebrews. Interestingly, he mentions the
    Apocalypse of John here once again: some reject it, but
    others include it in the recognized books.

It can be said that Hebrews was rejected in the West because
of its rejection of a second repentance, and the Apocalypse of
John in the East because of its lack of spirituality. In addition
there was controversy over the Catholic letters (except for
1 Peter and 1 John). The New Testament canon in its present
form, with twenty-seven books, is attested for the first time by
the thirty-ninth Easter festal letter of Metropolitan Athanasius
of Alexandria in 367. This is the canon at least in his sphere
of authority, Egypt, but after that it was no longer disputed.
Luther was the first to make an attempt to add the writings
which he criticized for theological reasons, namely Hebrews,
James, Jude and the Apocalypse, as a kind of appendix to the
New Testament: even now in Lutheran translations they stand
at the end of the New Testament, contrary to church tradition.

What were the motives for forming the canon? We have no
direct statements about them. Perhaps, however, an 'editorial'
by the editors of the New Testament has been preserved for
us in the New Testament in the form of 2 Peter. At least with
it we come relatively close to the time of the formation of the
canon. For 2 Peter is the latest writing in the New Testament.
It presupposes all parts of the canon (gospels, letters of
Paul and Catholic letters): 2 Peter 1.16ff. refers to the story of
the transfiguration in its Matthaean version and knows the
key term 'glory' from the Lukan version. 2 Peter 1.15 could
be a reference to the Gospel of Mark: 'Peter' assures his
readers that he wants to ensure that 'after my departure
you may be able at any time to recall these things (i.e. what
is good for life and piety)'. This could presuppose traditions like those in Papias, according to which Mark wrote
down the reminiscences of Peter. The Gospel of John, too,
is not unknown to 2 Peter. For 2 Peter knows a prophecy
of Peter's martyr death which occurs only in John 21.18–19

(2 Peter 1.14). He also mentions a collection of letters of Paul, the interpretation of which is disputed (3.16). And he knows at least one Catholic letter, 1 Peter (3.1). Possibly the expectation of a new heaven and a new earth (3.13) indicates knowledge of the Apocalypse (Rev. 21.1). Now in 2 Peter we can recognize two motives for the formation of the canon:

1. 2 Peter wants to guarantee a doctrine of the inspiration of scripture and control its exegesis: 'No prophecy of scripture is a matter of one's own interpretation, because no prophecy ever came by the impulse of man, but men moved by the Holy Spirit spoke from God' (1.20). It also adopts an attitude to the interpretation of the letters of Paul.

2. 2 Peter warns against false teachers. We hear of mockers who jest about the delay of the parousia. There are Christians who speak of the 'fathers'. Probably these are Christians who are close to gnosis, who understood the Christian faith spiritually and who could not cope with an expectation of the parousia understood literally. The New Testament canon came into being as a demarcation against false teachers.

But that is not the whole story. The great historical riddle of the formation of the canon is that in the second century there were no central government authorities in Christianity who could have established a canon of holy scriptures: there were no synods extending beyond regions, no bishop with an undisputed primacy, far less an emperor who was interested in the unity of Christianity. Nevertheless an amazing consensus developed without pressure. For apart from five Catholic letters, Hebrews and the Apocalypse, all the other writings formed a fixed canon in the second century. The many Gnostic writings were left out of account, although they made a high claim to revelation. Why did 'orthodox' writings like those of Ignatius and the letter of Barnabas remain outside the canon? It is clear that only writings of apostolic origin were accepted, but that does not explain why, say, the Teaching of the Apostles (the Didache) was not accepted.

Many of the Gnostic writings also claimed apostolic origin.
The consensus was based on criteria of content, on which
people were amazingly agreed. As a demarcation against
gnosis and Marcion two criteria became established: the unity
of God and the reality of the incarnation.

Any writing which taught a subordinate demiurge as creator
God alongside the true and transcendent God was rejected.
And this expressed a fundamental conviction: this world has
not been created by an ignorant or malicious demiurge, but
is in principle good. God's reason (his Logos) shapes it and
permeates it. At that time – in agreement with the Jewish–
Old Testament tradition – a decision was made to accept this
world in principle, however much it had been disfigured by
human failure. The unconditional yes to reality was expressed
in mythical form as repudiation of belief in a malicious creator
God.

Moreover, any writing was rejected which denied the complete incarnation – and accepted, say, the union of God with
only a higher part in human beings, or only a transitory union
of the divine and human natures in Christ, in other words a
'seeming' connection. So all these ideas can be summed up
under the term 'docetism' (= the doctrine of the 'semblance'
of the real existence of Jesus). Here too a fundamental
distinction broke through: the acceptance not just of the world
but of the whole of human life. If God (in the incarnation of
his Son) has taken human life upon himself unconditionally
– including corporeality and death – then the whole body
and the whole of human life is to be accepted, and nothing is
to be excluded from salvation. The unconditional yes to
human beings in all their existence was expressed in mythical
form as a fight against the docetic 'heresy'.

But what were the positive features of the faith of the first
Christians? What created in them that inner self-evidence
which made them prepared to sacrifice everything for Christ?
The writings of primitive Christianity are stamped with a
'spirit' that we recognize in a few basic motifs which keep
recurring. They need not be present in every work, but they
are like 'family resemblances', which always unite only limited
sub-groups. If religions are sign languages, these basic

motifs are the grammar of this language, the rules by which the signs are linked and organized. People who live in the world of the faith of the New Testament have internalized these motifs on the basis of the narratives and images of the New Testament, so that they spontaneously govern Christian action and experience. I shall end by compiling an open list of such basic motifs in the New Testament:

1. The *creation motif.* Everything could not have been and could have been different. A divine power which creates from nothing is active at every moment and enters history in the resurrection of Jesus.

2. The *wisdom motif.* The world has been created by God's wisdom, which shows itself in improbable structures, often veiled under their opposite – to the point of the 'folly' of the cross, in which God's wisdom is hidden.

3. The *motif of miracle.* Everything that happens is open to surprising turns; nothing is completely determined. God and human beings, faith and prayer bring about miraculous changes. Jesus is the bearer of such miraculous power.

4. The *motif of distance.* All life lives at a distance to God and does not correspond to the reality which has brought it forth and sustains it. In human beings this remoteness from God is made conscious through the experience of guilt and suffering: both separate it from God. In Christ God opens up this distance and overcomes it.

5. The *motif of hope and renewal.* A growing promise permeates history – to the point of the expectation of a new world which is already beginning now. Human beings are citizens of two worlds, imprisoned in the old world with their *sarx* (the flesh) and obligated to the new world which has begun with Jesus in the *pneuma* (the spirit).

6. The *motif of repentance.* Human beings have the possibility of radical change. Just as the world must change to correspond to God's will, so too must human beings –

they can begin a new life if they allow themselves to be crucified with Christ and with him begin a new life.

7. The *exodus motif.* Not only individuals but whole groups are changed by God's call – beginning with Abraham's exodus from his homeland and Israel's exodus from foreign lands and extending to the departure by the New Testament community for a new world as disciples of Jesus.

8. The *motif of faith.* God discloses himself through human beings whom we trust, i.e. not primarily through structures, institutions or ideas, but through a 'you' with whom we freely enter into a new relationship. At the centre of all the human beings through whom God speaks to us stands Jesus of Nazareth.

9. The *motif of incarnation.* God takes up his abode in the concrete world. He is present in Israel, in Christ, in the word, in the sacrament and in every believer through his spirit. The incarnation in Christ makes this nearness of God to human beings certain once and for all – even in guilt and suffering.

10. The *motif of representation.* Life is representative life for others – either life suffering unconsciously, at the cost of which other life unfolds, or deliberate life for others. The bloody animal sacrifices bear witness to the compulsion to live at the cost of others. Christ shows the alternative: life as surrender for others.

11. The *motif of change of position.* The first will be last and the last first. A transforming power goes forth from those who voluntarily renounce status to the point of self-stigmatization (in asceticism and martyrdom). And it goes forth even more from Christ, who as a judge was judged, as a priest became a sacrifice, as the ruler of the world became a slave, and as the crucified one became the basis of new life.

12. The *motif of agape.* Every fellow human being becomes our neighbour through love: whether through seeking the lost, welcoming the stranger or loving the enemy.

Here too Christ is the model for such love: the dedi-
cation of his life is love for those who were God's
'enemies'.

13. The *motif of judgment.* All life is subject to selective
    processes. Only human beings are aware of this; they
    know that they are threatened not only as physical living
    beings but also as moral agents. They are measured by
    what they have done – in accordance with ethical criteria
    according to which God passes a final judgment on
    them. Jesus is the criterion and judge.

14. The *motif of justification.* It is as impossible to fathom
    the legitimation of existence as it is to fathom the
    existence of life itself. Justification is a creation from
    nothing which human beings receive as receptively as
    they receive their physical existence. They have not
    created themselves. The basis of their justification is
    God's new creative action in Christ.

These fourteen basic motifs unite the most varied expres-
sions of primitive Christian faith: the Jesus tradition of the
synoptic gospels, the kerygmatic Christ of the letters, the
exclusive revealer of the Johannine writings. The same basic
motifs have their effect everywhere: in the synoptic narrative
of Jesus going around Galilee, proclaiming the kingdom of
God and seeking the lost; in the Pauline myth of the Son
of God who redeems human beings enslaved under sin and
death or in the Johannine fusion of the earthly Jesus with the
heavenly messenger. If human beings are seen in the light of
these motifs, they are given an unconditional value regardless
of status, origin, destiny and moral quality. Thus – in a
convergence with developments in the philosophy of the time
– this value of each individual is discovered. It remains
unconditional only when it is not grounded in conditioned
human beings.

These basic biblical motifs of action and experience were
at work in the primitive Christian groups. Christians and Jews
shared most of them, but Christians connected them closely
with the person of Jesus of Nazareth, whereas Jews derived

them from their biblical tradition. After the destruction of the temple, which had united them until AD 70, both groups had to develop into a religion of the book. In parallel to the canonization of the New Testament, in Judaism at the end of the second century the codified Mishnah, i.e. treatises which expounded the law, came into being. Both supplemented the Jewish Bible with further normative writings. Both are legitimate further developments of the Jewish Bible, which – from a historical perspective – has a later history on an equal footing in Judaism and Christianity, in the New Testament and the rabbinic literature. It was continued once again by Islam, which recognizes both the Old Testament and the New Testament as documents of revelation with a certain legitimacy. For many people a ray of eternity still shines from them in time. But it is worthwhile even for those who no longer hear these writings as preaching to read them and to immerse themselves in them. They are part of the fundamental cultural information of human history.

# Further Reading

### Introductions to the New Testament

R. E. Brown, *An Introduction to the New Testament*, Doubleday 1997

Etienne Charpentier, *How to Read the New Testament*, SCM Press and Crossroad Publishing Company 1981

Luke T. Johnson, *The Writings of the New Testament*, SCM Press and Fortress Press 1999

### Accounts of the literature, theology and religion of the New Testament

Helmut Koester, *Introduction to the New Testament* (2 vols), De Gruyter 1982

B. L. Mack, *Who Wrote the New Testament? The Making of the Christian Myth*, HarperCollins 1996

Gerd Theissen, *A Theory of Primitive Christian Religion*, SCM Press and Fortress Press 1999

### Jesus and the Jesus tradition

J. D. Crossan, *The Historical Jesus: The Life of a Mediterranean Jewish Peasant*, T&T Clark ²1993

E. P. Sanders, *The Historical Figure of Jesus*, Penguin Books 1995

E. P. Sanders, *Jesus and Judaism*, SCM Press and Fortress Press 1984

Dorothee Soelle and Luise Schottroff, *Jesus of Nazareth*, SPCK and Westminster Press 2002

Gerd Theissen, *The First Followers of Jesus*, SCM Press and Fortress Press 1978

Gerd Theissen, *The Shadow of the Galilean*, SCM Press 1987

Gerd Theissen and Annette Merz, *The Historical Jesus*, SCM Press and Fortress Press 1998

### Paul and the Pauline letters

Hans Frör, *You Wretched Corinthians!*, SCM Press 1995

J. Murphy-O'Connor, *Paul: A Critical Life*, Oxford University Press 1996

C. J. Roetzel, *Paul: The Man and the Myth*, Fortress Press 1999

E. P. Sanders, *Paul*, Oxford University Press 1991

D. Trobisch, *Paul's Letter Collection: Tracing the Origins*, Fortress Press 1994

### The logia source and the synoptic gospels

J. M. Robinson (ed.), *The Critical Edition of Q. Synopsis including the Gospels of Matthew and Luke, Mark and Thomas with English, German and French Translations of Q and Thomas*, Leuven 2000

E. P. Sanders and Margaret Davies, *Studying the Synoptic Gospels*, SCM Press and Fortress Press 1989

Wim Weren, *Windows on Jesus*, SCM Press 1999

### Pseudepigraphy

R. F. Collins, *Letters that Paul Did Not Write: The Epistle to the Hebrews and the Pauline Pseudepigrapha*, Michael Glazier 1988

D. G. Meade, *Pseudonymity and Canon: An Investigation into the Relationship of Authorship and Authority in Jewish and Early Christian Tradition*, Eerdmans 1986

### The Johannine writings

R. E. Brown, *The Community of the Beloved Disciple*, Paulist Press 1979

Oscar Cullmann, *The Johannine Circle*, SCM Press and Westminster Press 1976

Martin Hengel, *The Johannine Question*, SCM Press and Trinity Press International 1989

### The canon

H. F. von Campenhausen, *The Formation of the Christian Bible*, A&C Black and Fortress Press 1972

B. M. Metzger, *The Canon of the New Testament, Its Origin, Development and Significance*, Oxford University Press 1997

C. F. D. Moule, *The Birth of the New Testament*, A&C Black and Harper & Row 1982

# Glossary

**Apocalyptic**

Revelation literature, in which religious figures of the past (like Enoch, Abraham or Moses) are given knowledge about heavenly mysteries through visions or by being transported to heaven. This knowledge is especially about the end of time and about history up to the end of the world. Apocalyptic continues Old Testament prophecy in the post-exilic period.

**Apocrypha**

Writings which are related to the biblical writings but were not accepted into the canon. 'Apocrypha' literally means the 'hidden writings'.

**Beatitude**

Blessing (from the Latin). Occasionally called macarism (from the Greek *makarios* = happy).

***Bios***

Literally 'life'. The designation of ancient biography which does not do justice to our notions of biographies with an account of the development of a person from childhood to adulthood, and which therefore needs to be designated by a different term. A *bios* usually concentrates on the public activity of the hero.

## Canon

Literally 'guideline, measure'. A collection of writings which is the normative basis for the life and ethic of a religious community and its interpretation of the world. In the broader sense any writing appearing with a claim to religious authority seeks to be 'canonical'; in the narrower sense only writings which have been accepted into a binding list of a religious community are canonical writings.

## Charisma, charismatic

Literally 'gift of grace'. In primitive Christianity the term denotes an extraordinary gift of the spirit for the well-being of the community; in the modern social sciences it denotes any authority which rests on an irrational, personal force.

## Deutero-Pauline(s)

Literally 'only secondarily Pauline'. A designation for primitive Christian writings which have wrongly been attributed to Paul but which were written in the awareness of continuing his legacy: 2 Thessalonians, Colossians, Ephesians, 1 and 2 Timothy, Titus.

## Docetism

From the Greek *dokein* = 'appear'. The doctrine of an only apparent incarnation of God in Jesus. Docetism in the narrower sense assumes only an apparent body, which just looked like a body. Docetism in the wider sense assumes a transitory association between a real body and a divine being which is done away with again before death.

## Epiphany

Appearance of a deity, often accompanied by miraculous phenomena.

## Eschatology, eschatological

Literally 'teaching about the last things' (*eschatos* = last). All notions of an end of the world or a fundamental overcoming of the existing world in the present are called 'eschatological'. The term 'present eschatology' is used to denote an end which dawns in history, and 'future eschatology' to denote an end which is expected in the future.

## Essenes

From the Hebrew Hassidim = 'pious'. The designation of a group of pious in Judaism who are mentioned in the sources alongside the two other great 'parties' of the Pharisees and Sadducees. The settlement at Qumran by the Dead Sea, which has been excavated, is usually now regarded as their centre, though not all Essenes lived there.

## Glossolalia

Speaking in tongues, a phenomenon widespread in primitive Christianity (and in the present-day Pentecostal movement), in which meaningless noises are made. In the account of Pentecost glossolalia is interpreted as 'xenologia', i.e. speaking in foreign languages. However, that is a secondary interpretation which does not fit glossolalia either in primitive Christianity or in the present.

## Gnosis

Literally 'knowledge'. A religious current which emerges fully in the second century AD and combines a radical repudiation of the world (as the work of a subordinate and incompetent demiurge) with a radically high view of the self (the inner self is part of the divine world). It teaches that redemption is possible through an intuitive knowledge of the inner self.

## Gospel

Literally 'good news'. It originally denotes the oral proclamation of a change in the direction of salvation and is secondarily transferred to the writings which tell of Jesus as the bringer of this turning point. From being a term denoting proclamation the word became the designation of a literary genre.

### Hellenism

The designation of Greek culture which spread through the East after Alexander the Great and there interacted intensively with the native oriental cultures.

### Judaizers

Jewish Christians who in the first century AD worked towards making all Christians Jews and accepting circumcision and the regulations about food.

### Kerygma, kerygmatic

Literally 'proclamation'. In exegetical terminology this denotes above all the proclamation of Christ, of God's action in his cross and resurrection, as distinct from the proclamation of the historical Jesus.

### Logion (pl. logia)

Literally 'word, saying'. A designation for short sayings of Jesus.

### Magnificat

The first word (in Latin) of Mary's song of praise in Luke 1.46–55 and therefore a name for the whole hymn.

### Messiah

Literally 'the anointed'. In the New Testament period a designation for an expected saving figure who is occasionally expected as a priest, more frequently as a prophet, but usually as a king who will free Israel from foreign rule and restore it. Anointing was once a coronation ritual. Hence the name 'anointed'.

### Mishnah

Hebrew 'repetition'. The name for the oral Torah in Judaism; it was set down in writing around the end of the second century AD and became an ingredient of the Talmud.

**Monotheism**

Belief in only one God and the denial of the existence of any other gods. By contrast, 'monolatry' means the exclusive worship of a God without denying the existence of other gods.

**Myth**

Literally 'narrative'. As a rule narratives of how superhuman agents (gods, demons, angels) shape the world decisively in the primal period (or also in the end time). How people are to act ethically, and how they are to worship the gods ritually, emerges from myth.

**Paraclete**

A term for the 'Holy Spirit' which occurs only in the Gospel of John. Literally 'the one who is summoned', Latin *advocatus*, defender and comforter. The Johannine Jesus first uses this term in the Johannine farewell discourses for the Holy Spirit, which he promises as a substitute for his presence.

**Paraenesis, paraenetic**

Literally encouragement, admonition. Ethical instruction in the form of a series of imperatives or admonitions.

**Parousia**

Literally 'presence' or 'arrival'. In the New Testament it denotes the arrival (as a return) of Jesus, which initially is expected imminently. The experience that this arrival of Jesus failed to materialize is designated 'delay of the parousia'.

**Pentateuch**

Literally 'five volumes'. Designation for the five books of Moses.

**Pericope**

Literally 'section'. Sections of the Bible which are the basis for an exposition or a reading. In the gospels these are often originally independent 'small units' which could be handed down independently of one another.

## Pseudepigraphy

Literally 'false attribution'. Writings which are published or circulated under false names are pseudepigraphical writings.

## Revelation scheme

A notion which often occurs in post-Pauline letters (Rom. 6.25–27; Col. 1.26–27; Eph. 3.4–5; 1 Peter 1.20; 2 Tim. 1.9–10) that God's plan of salvation was hidden for a long time and has only been manifested in Christ. Here the Old Testament as a time of revelation seems to have been passed over.

## Synoptics

The first three gospels, Matthew, Mark and Luke, are called 'synoptics' or 'synoptic gospels'. Since they are related, they can be 'seen together' and printed for a comparison in a 'synopsis' divided into three columns. 'Synopsis' literally means 'see together'.

# Index of Biblical References